THE SEED

INFERTILITY IS A FEMINIST ISSUE

ALEXANDRA KIMBALL

COACH HOUSE BOOKS, TORONTO

Published with the generous assistance of the Canada Council for the Arts and the Ontario Arts Council. Coach House Books also gratefully acknowledges the support of the Government of Canada through the Canada Book Fund and the Government of Ontario through the Ontario Book Publishing Tax Credit.

LIBRARY AND ARCHIVES CANADA CATALOGUING IN PUBLICATION

Title: The seed : infertility is a feminist issue / Alexandra Kimball.
Names: Kimball, Alexandra, 1978- author.
Series: Exploded views.
Description: Series statement: Exploded views
Identifiers: Canadiana (print) 20190053097 | Canadiana (ebook) 20190053135 | ISBN 9781552453858 (softcover) | ISBN 9781770565913 (EPUB) | ISBN 9781770565920 (PDF)
Subjects: LCSH: Infertility, Female. | LCSH: Infertility, Female—Social aspects. | LCSH: Infertility, Female—Psychological aspects. | LCSH: Reproductive rights. | LCSH: Feminism.
Classification: LCC RG201 .K56 2019 | DDC 618.1/78—dc23

The Seed is available as an ebook: ISBN 978 1 77056 385 8 (EPUB), ISBN 978 1 77056 591 3 (PDF).

Purchase of the print version of this book entitles you to a free digital copy. To claim your ebook of this title, please email sales@chbooks.com with proof of purchase. (Coach House Books reserves the right to terminate the free download offer at any time.)

Introduction

One afternoon in the summer of 2017, around when I hit the nadir of my struggle with infertility, I arrived early for a therapy appointment and decided to kill time at a local park. The park was deeply shaded – it felt easy to get lost in. On a nearby bench, a man reclined with his head on a ripped knapsack, a cigarette in one dangling hand, and behind a hedge, two teenagers smoked weed, tinny music playing on one of their phones. The two kinds of smoke mingled, dirty-sweet.

On the sidewalk bisecting the park, a woman had stopped with her toddler son. 'Bub bub,' he said, looking at me, pointing with one chubby hand. His mother, a woman about my age, tugged on the boy's other hand, trying to get him to move along, but he stayed put. 'Bub bub,' he said again – insistently but without any distress. Above his squinted eyes, his faint eyebrows were scrunched. It was an expression of benign resolve, like that of a teacher or bureaucrat tasked with making a point.

'Sorry,' the woman mouthed apologetically, and I smiled at her, to let her know it was okay. She returned my smile. She had blondish hair pushed back in a ponytail and an ass-centric chubbiness that looked a little awkward – a new and unfamiliar body, after recently giving birth. The muchness of her! With a stroller ahead of her, a swollen knap-sack on her back, and the child attached to her hand, she spread across almost the entire sidewalk, fore and aft, a whole ecosystem. I knew from mothers I'd talked with that there wasn't much comfort in taking up so much space: they felt hypervisible, objects of public scrutiny. But still, they never failed to transfix me. How having a baby seemed to multiply a woman, adding to her not only baby but also baby-stuff; not only enlarging her, but also rooting her to the ground. In contrast, I felt insubstantial, wafting around a park at four on a Monday, shaded by leaves and smoke.

There was a part of me that was surprised they could even see me. Four and a half years and four miscarriages into infer-tility, I had become very good at being ephemeral. When I was not writing from home, or disappearing into the closed-off exam rooms of fertility clinics, I was online, in any of a dozen or so infertility and miscarriage groups where women like me gathered for advice and support. Yet even though I spent so much time connected to these other invisible women, our connection was so specific, and in such isolation from the rest of our lives, that it felt ultimately tenuous. We knew each other only as diagnoses; as one thing. I often thought of some-thing Nigerian feminist Chimamanda Ngozi Adichie has said about the single story, and where it leads: 'The single story creates stereotypes, and the problem with stereotypes is not that they are untrue, but that they are incomplete. They make one story become the only story.'

If there is a single story of infertile women, its theme is isolation. In roughly half of all cases of infertility – defined by the World Health Organization as a reproductively aged, oppo-site-sex couple's failure to conceive after a year of unprotected intercourse – the cause can be traced to the male partner. Men suffer emotionally and socially from infertility as well as physically; studies have shown that infertile men experience double the rates of depression and anxiety as their fertile peers. The masculinist ideal, which links manliness not only to virility but to stoicism, compounds men's distress: infertile men tend to disclose their experiences to friends and family members less than their female partners do, with the consequence that they are especially deprived of social validation and support. And yet, the psychological and social burden of infertility is borne largely by women. A review of couples who visited a Swedish fertility clinic found that female patients were at twice the risk as male patients for a major psychiatric disorder at the conclusion of treatment, with special stress in areas of social, sexual, and relationship adjustment. (Multiple other studies have found these risks are higher in childless women compared to those who had previously conceived, and in women with three or more years of infertility compared to fewer, and can remain elevated in women up to twenty years after the conclusion of treatment.) Which is to say that the additional stress of infertility knocks us into a distinct category of psychological concern. In one famous 1993 study, the psychological symptoms of infertile women were compared to those of women diagnosed with other life-altering conditions; their stress levels were found to be equal to those of women living with cancer. Infertile women who are childless are at particular risk: a Danish metastudy found that childless female fertility-clinic patients were 47 per cent more likely to be hospitalized for schizophrenia over their lifetime than patients who eventually gave birth.

This divide between the male and female experience of infertility is no doubt due in part to an unavoidable physical distinction: it is far more invasive, time-consuming, costly, and risky to diagnose and/or treat issues of the internal ovaries or uterus than it is problems originating in the testes. Even for many straight couples facing sperm issues, the only way to conceive may be through in-vitro fertilization (IVF), a procedure that requires a sperm sample from the man, while the woman must endure a month of drugs and monitoring, as well as egg retrieval, which requires minor surgery. But beyond the greater physical commitment, women also take on the social responsibility of infertility. The past century has seen a great expansion of the things that women worldwide are (at least legally) allowed to do and be, but the traditional link between womanhood and motherhood is seemingly intractable. Writing in the *New York Times*, 'ex-infertile' Shelagh Little explains:

> Motherhood is still central to womanhood, the magical thing that women's bodies do. Motherhood is also socially rewarded and is a sort of proxy for femininity. In candid moments, mothers tell you that they liked being pregnant because of all the attention they got. As an infertile, I feel oddly unsexed, especially when I look at pregnant women. I cannot do that (be pregnant), so am I still really a woman? (That's a hypothetical.)

Sociologists call it the 'motherhood mandate'; on Pinterest it appears as a meme by feminist folksinger Ani DiFranco: 'birth is the epicenter of women's power.' Against this backdrop, it's far from surprising that, for women, infertility manifests itself not just as personal shame but as confusion and existential grief. Infertile women report their greatest stress around the social aspects of infertility, including a feeling of disruption in the normal life trajectory, stigmatization, and what Little terms a 'meaning vacuum.' As maternity is (still) supposed to provide a woman's life with meaning, informing and shaping everything else in her life, the infertile woman is excluded from the accepted symbolic order of feminine life. 'Infertility,' Little writes, 'is a unique kind of loneliness.' Misogynist stereotypes and stigma isolate women with infertility and prevent us from speaking publicly about our experiences. And yet, infertility has never been fully understood as an issue for women as a class, let alone as a feminist issue.

As I mused over some artifact of my isolation – how disconnected I felt from my online infertility groups; why I felt I couldn't tell other people we were struggling to conceive – I often thought back to my experience of having had an abortion in my mid-twenties. How it was...well, if not pleasant, exactly, about as untraumatic as having an unwanted fetus sucked out through my cervix could be. Unlike what I was going through with infertility, my abortion did not rock my sense of self: I emerged from it intact. This wasn't inevitable. In previous decades, women who sought abortions, especially young, unmarried women like I was, were only one thing: sluts. But by the time I slid into the stirrups, the women's movement had been working for decades to not only ensure that abortion was safe and accessible, but to humanize the women who got them. For the 1990s era, third-wave feminist culture I came of age with, the demonizing of women who had abortions was almost as tragic as the policy that restricted access to them. The stereotypes around abortion-seeking had been shaped by eons of stigma, and had the potential to affect multiple areas of a woman's life. In addition to their tireless and often dangerous work countering policies that restricted safe abortion, feminist actors disseminated literature about abortion, collected data, and provided visible support to female patients. Some laudable organizations even matched abortion patients with volunteers so that vulnerable women did not have to navigate the experience alone. This continues today, bolstered by digital abortion activism. On a grassroots level, both in-person and online groups exist to help women process their experiences with abortion, teasing out the ways in which their experiences might also be shaped by other realities of their lives, like race and sexuality and class.

During the months around my own abortion, I frequented one group like this online. There was a galvanizing, seventies-ish vibe I found healing. We discussed things like whether or not speculums needed to be so medieval; we wondered what terminating a pregnancy might be like if the procedure had been designed by female doctors. At the heart of all our conversations was a deeper questioning of the isolation and shame that traditionally marked women who had abortions. Several other women who participated in these chats went on to political work, trying to improve policy that would help women gain access to safe abortions and feel supported.

Coming from the world of abortion to the world of infertility, I felt like I had jetted back in time. While researching this book, I posted a question on a few message boards, asking for stories from other infertile women about how feminism may have affected their experiences with infertility. Two groups removed the post as violating a rule of 'no politics allowed.'

In *The Experience of Infertility*, one of the few books on infertility written by infertile women, authors Naomi Pfeffer and Anne Woollett describe how the dominant view of infertility as primarily a medical problem effectively erased women's own experiences. At the time of publication, 1983, the existing information on infertility was all 'from the doctor's point of view.' These texts give us a lot of information about the mechanics of the tests [but] do not say how it feels to undergo them, whether they hurt, or are emotionally upsetting. Because our experiences do not match the perspectives of the doctor, we feel that we are somehow bizarre or unusual.

Pfeffer and Woollett go on to attribute the paucity of women-centred infertility literature to the lack of attention to infertility within the women's movement:

These feelings of isolation were accentuated for us because, as feminists, we had expected to be able to talk to other women, to be able to discuss our infertility within a feminist context. But we found the taboos and silence on infertility just as strong within the women's movement. This made us feel sad and sometimes very angry. It denied the reality of our experience … Margaret Sanger, a pioneer of birth control, wrote … 'No woman can call herself free until she can choose consciously whether she will or will not be a mother.' But this right to choose is defined in terms of the right not to have children. The right to have children…is much less considered. Even further down this list of 'priorities' are the rights of infertile women whose experiences and needs remain largely invisible.

Though written decades earlier, this book became one of the few texts on infertility that accurately captured my experience. I felt a sense of double alienation: on the one hand, from an infertility community that rejected feminism, and on the other, from a feminism that ignored and misunderstood the lives of infertile women. If the former consigned my infertility to a stereotype, to one thing, the latter had reduced it to no thing at all.

Seeing women like the mother in the park would heighten my sense of difference and isolation, but so too would women like my childless-by-choice, feminist female friends who posted memes like 'resistance is fertile' on Twitter, and rallied every year at SlutWalk and the Women's March. I don't go to events like this anymore, but every so often I'll spend a whole afternoon looking at photos of them online, feeling envious and admiring and bitter all at once. The crowds of women occupying space, and the novelty of this. The muchness of them! Flushed faces overlaid by signs: 'My Body, My Choice.' Women holding babies in carriers holding their own signs: 'Future Feminist.' Feminist mothers – these were the hardest to look at.

I wondered what these women knew about infertility, and what they thought about infertile women like me. Whether they felt that 'choice' extended to women like me, who wanted kids but couldn't have them. Whether, like many feminists, they thought surrogacy and egg donation – advanced technologies we were pursuing – meant the de facto enslaving of poor women by privileged white women like me. There were always women in these crowds holding signs referencing the TV version of *The Handmaid's Tale* – had they noticed how, in its world view, feminine infertility is equated with feminine evil, and the only 'real' mothers are those who give birth?

Statistically, at least one in five of those feminist mothers had once struggled to conceive. They knew the pain of longing and isolation, the song of infertility, even if it wasn't something they talked about a lot now, or thought to write on a sign. I wondered if I had encountered any of them before, in the waiting rooms of fertility clinics, or in online groups where women talked about their follicle counts, and how many embryos their doctors told them to expect, and how alone they felt. We may have passed each other without recognition, without impacting each other, ephemeral.

The irony here was profound. If I, as an infertile person, felt insubstantial, the work of infertility – to process and cope with thwarted longing, and to build, in some cases, a family – was solid. More than that, it was bodily – often in the sense of prolonged medical labour, but always through the physical transformations on the level of one's muscles, hormones, and fat cells that remake infertile women into animals that have survived grief. And whether or not we disclosed our infertility, we were also doing social and emotional work, reconfiguring every relationship that branched out from that central, unrealized dyad of us-plus-child. That the work of infertility only sometimes produced children did not make it less productive. Resolved or not, recognized or not, infertility, just like pregnancy, always forged new women with new inner and outer worlds.

I started researching this book as a way to find words for an experience for which few seemed to exist – what Virginia Woolf, writing about illness, called a 'poverty of the language ... a state of mind which neither words can express nor the reason explain.' But what I found was, in fact, that not only were representations of infertility everywhere, they suffused everything. Narratives of infertility were the manna in which every other story about women took shape: every tale about what it means to be a woman, about what women's work is and does, and how we should or could become mothers. How beneath every story of a woman and a child was the unspoken threat of a woman without a child, longing for a child. Considered with one eye to feminist history, this erasure is functionally systematic: the refusal of feminist policy and culture to recognize and support the labour of infertile women mirrors and upholds its refusal to recognize and support other women doing other kinds of work, in different and even less visible margins. In this sense, the story of infertility vis-à-vis feminism speaks to a broader difficulty the women's movement has had with difference among women, and how we are to deal with this difference while still having one another's backs – a greater struggle with inclusivity.

Ultimately, while I had been disappointed in what feminism had had to say about female infertility, I found that, once located, what infertility had to say about feminism was expansive and provocative – productive. My challenge was less about articulating the ephemeral than about uncovering: finding where female infertility was hidden in all the stories we're often told about women, old and new, normative and feminist. To dig it out – to try to see what other stories it might suggest once unearthed. It was not so different from the work I was doing as an infertile woman and, later, as an expectant mother, and then, finally, as a new parent. As with all birth projects, what follows is an exercise in differentiation, in untangling old and fused roots.

One

The summer after our third miscarriage, Jeremy convinced me to go to a fancy party for his work. He thought that dressing up and eating a nice meal in a ballroom with other dressed-up people might distract me. I sat in my cocktail dress – too tight on my post-IVF bloat – and held my husband's hand under the table. Occasionally a waiter would pass by with canapés and I'd grab one with my free hand. The table was buzzing with wine-leavened conversation, with introductions and interruptions and compliments, especially for the women, who wore a lot of black and navy, modest necklines, the assured unchic of women who do not need to impress. They generated an air of capability and confidence, success.

I desperately, desperately did not want to talk to any of them. Over the past four years, socializing had become my biggest problem, second only to infertility. If you had asked me about my social life, I would have said, 'It does not exist,' though, in fact, all I did was talk to other people, in online support groups on Facebook and the forum sections of infertility websites. I'd wake up in the morning and log on and read and write all day with hundreds of infertile women, sharing details of our miscarriages, our IVF results, our search for a surrogate, and reply to their queries and stories in turn. But as soon as I logged off, I'd forget all about them. Not to say I found these groups useless – if I wasn't happy about my condition, I was certainly grateful to have a place I could discuss it. But the occasion of these conversations left them feeling ghostly and unreal, in a way that talking with other women, even about other shitty and gendered topics, never had. The discussions in these forums seemed less like genuine attempts at conversation than they did like monologues, or the petitions ancient women used to inscribe on tablets, one by one, in front of oracles for Artemis and Zeus: *Will there be children for me?*

Part of this was inevitable, I thought: it's difficult for someone so deep into her own suffering to connect with anyone else, let alone someone who is suffering just as much. But I also wondered about what I felt was a deeply unfeminist, even antifeminist, vibe at work in these spaces. Not because we were all struggling to have children, which, duh, is the number one edict of patriarchy, and not even because the majority of posters were not interested in feminism or politics (in fact, a significant number appeared to be right-wing Christian women). Rather, it's that these groups are set up to benefit the individual infertile woman, as opposed to infertile women as a group. Regardless of the banner art on every page that urged members to support infertility research, or the white ribbons to which we dutifully changed our avatars every October to coincide with Infertility Awareness Month, posters rarely discussed 'ending infertility.' The purpose of these groups was not communal, it was individual – each member was there to figure out how she, personally, could have a baby. And once she did, it was rare to hear from her again. (Some groups have a separate section for infertile women who have successfully conceived – in one forum, this section was literally titled 'The Other Side.')

Still, the outside world – I thought of anything non-infertility-related as 'outside' and still do – was way worse. Somewhere along the four-year way, my outside friends – all feminists, all solidarity- and collective-minded – had retreated. I'd see them every once in a while, but they felt remote, far-off in their own galaxies of pregnancy, baby-raising, or simply just not being infertile. I backed off, too. Not infrequently, I'd think of one of these women and feel a sudden hurt, but I preferred this pain to the sharp vertigo I experienced whenever they said something to remind me of my new difference, my distance. Social life presented an agonizing conundrum: my infertility was the only thing in my life, and no one apart from other infertile women ever wanted to talk about it.

At Jeremy's work party, I was trying to silently project a sense of my private agony, but eventually, the woman seated beside me tapped me on the hand and asked me my name. She was older than me, maybe fiftyish, with a coiffed bob and a pale pink satin pantsuit that was frivolous enough to suggest that maybe she wasn't one of the many lawyers, but a lawyer's wife. I hoped not, because the wives always asked me about kids. Which she did.

'Do you have any kids?'

'No,' I said.

'Do you plan on having them?' she asked. Her expression was quizzical, slightly amused.

'We can't,' I said. 'We've had three miscarriages.'

Despite being clinical, correct, the word *miscarriage*, like the word *infertility*, always suggests the particular unruliness of the female body – a mess of genitals and organs. And even given the culture's nominal feminism (I would be shocked if any woman at that party would have rejected being labelled a feminist), there is a perpetual undercurrent of disgust about female genitals and organs. They are, in the words of French surrealist Michel Leiris, 'unclean or as a wound … but dangerous in itself, like everything bloody, mucous, infected.'

Saying 'miscarriage' out loud was like putting my uterus on the table, bleeding and scarred and radiating misuse. Tears and death and not a small amount of sex. I felt vulgar, dropping this bit of feminine gore into the lighthearted civility of the room. I understood the irony: I had no more exposed my uterus by talking about my lack of children than any other woman who mentions 'having kids.' All children, living or dead, come from bloody uteruses and vaginas – things polite people don't discuss – but the logic of misogyny, which carves out a space of relative respect for some mothers (especially the wealthy, white, and married), means we usually agree to forget this. The beauty of the child erases its origins in the female body and sexuality. But when these parts go wrong and there is no child, nothing is redeemed. It's just the spectre of the female body and sexuality: blood, mucous, infection. Death.

A few moments passed. The woman's mouth opened and closed over the empty air. The waiter came by again, and I plucked a canapé from a round tray. Open, closed, open, closed, like she was gulping air.

'Oh,' she finally said, before rushing off, to the washroom or something – I didn't see her again. I still don't know who she was. Her chair remained empty all night, and whenever I looked at it, I wanted to laugh. It was funny, really: a literal instantiation of my isolation. Like my infertility was creating a force field around me. Suddenly the distance I felt from my outside friends snapped into sense: *infertility has a lot of power.*

When TV and movies want to underscore an infertile female character's isolation, they send her to an oblivious friend's baby shower. But in my digital support groups, a more common scenario is that we do not get invited to baby showers; in fact, our friends who are pregnant or parenting small children begin avoiding us altogether. Infertile women will often find out about our friends' and even relatives' pregnancies, baby showers, and births on Facebook, after the fact. Writing on pregnancy loss, American sociologists Wendy Simonds and Barbara Katz Rothman identify this isolation as the primary theme in all literature on miscarriage: 'Bereaved mothers say, again and again, no one wanted to hear, no one let me talk, no one listened, no one said "I'm sorry." It happened in silence.'

Discussing the topic in her excellent *Motherhood Lost: A Feminist Account of Pregnancy Loss in America*, anthropologist Linda L. Layne quotes a woman whose experiences are typical:

> [P]eople shied away either because they didn't know what to say or because it could be a reality for them that they couldn't deal with … [F]eelings of loneliness … began to sink in. People who knew what had happened either ignored me or said something inappropriate.

Feeling rejected by outside friends was one of the only non-medical topics that got much play in my online support groups (more so even than marital problems, which, surprisingly, I didn't see discussed much). Posters spent a lot of time trying to decipher their friends' motives.

'I know she didn't want to hurt my feelings,' one woman wrote, after discovering that her sister-in-law had not issued her a baby-shower invitation. Or maybe, she wrote, she simply didn't know how to respond to her relative's pain and loss, and was trying to avoid the awkwardness and discomfort an infertile woman at a baby shower would present. She wanted justification, and the other women in the group all gave it; we wrote that the sister-in-law was not being malicious, that she was just ignorant, that she was trying to spare the woman's feelings. But we all felt the slap, having weathered these slights ourselves. However benign the reason for excluding us, the effect was always that we felt immediately othered, so identified with the tragedy of infertility that we had become impossible to relate to, let alone socialize with. We knew that our suffering was unimaginable to most women, and that the very fact of us was frightening and depressing and better when just ignored. We had become monsters, like the one Mary Shelley's Dr. Frankenstein creates – 'solitary and abhorred.'

I felt my difference, my solitariness and despicability, most keenly at that dinner, but it took several more encounters (more 'I don't know what to say,' more ignored requests, more absent party invitations) for me to start thinking that the horror of my infertility – my monstrousness – was not just about how different I was from regular, fertile women, but also how similar, how close. I imagined that the women who avoided me were very invested in having children (or more children) themselves. They retreated from me because they saw me as a worst-case scenario, a personal nightmare – even an omen. Monsters blur categories: human and beast; living and dead; man and woman. With fecundity so tied to femininity, I often sensed how my infertility desexed me, how it rendered me both female and not-quite female in a way that was not just sad but unsettling. The best monsters – vampires, zombies, aliens – are uncanny perversions of the human, recognizable in some form as us. ('[M]y form is a filthy type of yours,' says Frankenstein's monster, 'more horrid even from the very resemblance.') The threat of the monster isn't death, it's contamination – that they might infect us with their abomination and turn us into monsters as well. When other women avoided me, I wondered if they believed, on some level, that my infertility was contagious, and that by dealing with me, they might have to contend with their fear that they might be infertile, too.

From her first recorded mentions the infertile female was a monster, distinct from woman-proper. The Babylonian Atrahasis epic, from the eighteenth-century BCE, describes a conflict between the gods and the overpopulated, lazy world of men, during which the gods flooded the earth. Eventually repenting for this destruction, the deities restored humankind to the earth, with a built-in safeguard against overpopulation: 'Let there be a third group of people. [Let there be] fertile women and barren women. Let there be the "Eradicator" among the people and let her snatch the child from the lap of the mother.' The Eradicator was the lion-headed demoness Lamashtu, barren and envious, who caused infertility, miscarriage, and infant death among the populace. She could only be warded off by reciting all of her seven names. Yet her existence is essential to the flourishing fertility of the population at large – the infertility of some women is the price Babylonians paid for the fertility of most. Lamashtu is an explicit early example of how the fear and Othering of female infertility is foundational to society's functioning.

The Hebrew Testament of Solomon describes the demon Abyzou – her name derived from the word for abyss – as a fusion of woman and beast: 'her glance was altogether bright and greeny, and her hair was tossed wildly like a dragon's; and the whole of her limbs were invisible.' Abyzou was barren, and she confessed that her envy of women who could bear children motivated her murderous hauntings:

> [B]y night I sleep not, but go my rounds over all the world, and visit women in childbirth … [I]f I am lucky, I strangle

the child. But if not, I retire to another place. For I cannot for a single night retire unsuccessful. For I am a fierce spirit, of myriad names and many shapes. And now hither, now thither I roam ... I have no work other than the destruction of children, and the making their ears to be deaf, and the working of evil to their eyes, and the binding their mouths with a bond, and the ruin of their minds, and paining of their bodies.

Considered the cause of stillbirths and miscarriage, Abyzou was likely the source of child-killing monsters in other antiquity cultures: the Jewish Lilith, the Egyptian Alabasandria, and the Byzantine Gylou. The art of the period depicts these demons as serpentine, the unruly, unnatural appearance of such female forms evoking their barrenness and symbolizing their rebuke to traditional femininity. Accordingly, they were often painted being trampled under male riders on horses, a triumph of the masculine state order over the vengeful, inchoate feminine. Amulets depicting such figures were used by pregnant women to ward off vengeful spirits.

In Indonesia, a tree-dwelling spirit named Wewe Gombel was similarly motivated to evil deeds by her infertility. In life, Wewe Gombel's husband committed infidelity when he learned she was barren, and, upon discovering this, she murdered him. The villagers drove her from the village, and she killed herself. In her spirit form, she devoted herself to making up the family she could not have, kidnapping unsupervised children and confining them in her palm tree, where she enchanted them into staying. Engravings depict her as naked and dishevelled, with matted hair and outsized, pendulous breasts (some stories have her using her breasts to hide the stolen children as she spirits them away). In folk tales, parents use her vengeful presence to warn their children against straying too far or misbehaving, a cautionary tale that figures the barren female as the ultimate threat to orderly family life, spreading her childlessness to others. She is symbolically linked to the early Hindu goddess Nirrti, who was responsible for miscarriages, infertility, and child abductions, as well as general death and decay; in a culture where infertility was presumed to always be the result of female disorder, and punishable by not only divorce but exile and death, women prayed frequently to ward off Nirrti's influence.

In the Middle Ages, the Abyzou archetype informed the European idea of the witch, frequently accused of kidnapping children and causing miscarriages and stillbirths. The witch burnings in Europe and North America were a touchstone for late-twentieth-century feminist historians, who rightfully noted how the accused (of which around 80 per cent were female) often defied the conventional female gender roles of the era: many were unmarried, for example, or exhibited the unwomanly characteristics of anger or promiscuity. But fewer have emphasized how prominently female barrenness figured in the witch trials, how infertile and childless women were considered both particularly vulnerable to infestation by Satanic spirits and prone to acts of witchcraft themselves. More broadly, witchcraft itself manifested in the form of barrenness of all living things: miscarriages (both human and animal), famines, droughts, and crop wastages. The horror of infertility permeates the first Papal Bull on witchcraft in 1484:

> Many persons of both sexes, unmindful of their own salva-
> tion, and straying from the Catholic faith, have abandoned
> themselves to devils, incubi, and succubi, and by their
> incantations, spells, conjurations, and other accursed

charms and crafts, enormities and horrid offences, have slain infants yet in the mother's womb, as also the offspring of cattle, have blasted the produce of the earth, the grapes of the vine ... they hinder men from performing the sexual act and women from conceiving, whence husbands cannot know their wives nor wives receive their husbands ... they do not shrink from committing and perpetrating the foulest abominations and filthiest excesses to the deadly peril of their own souls.

Many of the highest-profile witchcraft trials centred on infertile women. Even as childlessness was presumed to be the result of female infertility alone, a common assumption during this period was that male impotence was caused by female sorcery (itself an effect of a woman having sex with the Devil). In 1754 in São Paulo, Brazil, Ursulina de Jesus was accused of using sorcery to render the couple infertile, and her resulting trial and execution by burning was one of Brazil's most sensational witchcraft cases. Her husband later failed to conceive children with his second wife, indicating that he had been responsible for the couple's barrenness – a potent example of how medieval theology constructed female infertility as a scapegoat for larger concerns about masculine virility. In Puritan North America, a childless woman, Eunice 'Goody' Cole, was accused in 1656 of witchcraft by neighbours, who blamed her for the death of local livestock. Described by historian Joseph Dow as 'ill-natured and ugly, artful and aggravating, malicious and revengeful,' Cole was imprisoned and tortured several times over a period of ten years, earning the title of 'the Witch of Hampton' (she still figures prominently in local legends; Hampton, Massachusetts, has a diner named after her). The spectre of infertility even condemned women who were in fact fertile, as happened in the seventeenth-century trial of German wife Merga Bien. An argumentative woman who had been in a childless marriage for fourteen years, Bien was first arrested on suspicion of attending Satanic rites, but convicted when it was discovered that she was pregnant. Inquisitors believed such fertility after prolonged barrenness could only be the result of demonic intervention, and Bien was executed in 1603.

The Old and New Testaments had, on their surface, a good deal of sympathy for infertile women (the invocation 'Sing, O barren woman!' compares the plight of the chosen people of Israel to the sorrow of an infertile wife). But her potential for danger is always present, troubling that male sympathy. The barren monsters of pagan myth and folklore were threatening not only because they defied the edict for women to procreate, but because each of these feminine demons demonstrated her anger and bitterness over her situation, which fuelled her acts of supernatural revenge. As in these tales, the Bible defined women as passive instruments of their reproductive fate; the standard woman was 'self-controlled, pure, working at home, kind, and submissive to their own husbands' (Titus 2:4-5). Thus emerged the only acceptable image of the infertile woman: the pining religious supplicant, symbolized most strikingly in the Biblical story of Hannah. Infertile but virtuous, she is first encountered in a moment of submission, having skipped food and drink at a family gathering to pray to God for a (specifically, male) child:

> 'O Lord of Hosts, if You will look upon the suffering of Your maidservant and will remember me and not forget Your maidservant, and if You will grant Your maidservant a male child, I will dedicate him to the Lord for all the

days of his life, and there shall no razor come upon his head.' (1 Samuel 1:11)

Hannah is praying silently, unwilling to disturb others with her distress, which causes the priest Eli to interrupt and accuse her of drunkenness. Hannah rehearses her predicament in terms that also underscore her feminine piety:

'Oh no, my lord! I am a very unhappy woman. I have drunk no wine or other strong drink, but I have been pouring out my heart to the Lord. Do not take your maidservant for a worthless woman; I have only been speaking all this time out of my great anguish and distress.' (1 Samuel 1:14–15)

Hannah's story circumscribes acceptable attitude for the infertile woman – prayer, silence, submission, and acceptance of God's will. Rabbis of the period believed that barrenness existed 'because the Holy One, blessed be He, longs to hear the prayer of the righteous'; at the same time, barren women had little to no social status and female infertility was grounds for divorce. Unsurprisingly, Hannah's is the only prayer by a woman recorded in the Bible, illustrating the proper response to female infertility as it underscores the importance of prayer and the centrality of God to the mysteries of reproduction. (In Psalm 13: 'He makes the barren woman abide in the house As a joyful mother of children. Praise the Lord!') And it also invokes her propriety: after Eli tells her to 'go in peace' and resume eating and drinking, 'she is happy.' Spoiler alert: God eventually gives Hannah a (male) baby. She is one of the earliest examples of the enduring cliché that if a woman has enough faith (or, in our secular cult of 'wellness,' is 'positive' enough), a miracle pregnancy is all but inevitable. In my digital infertility groups, a meme is often posted beneath stories of the poorest prognoses: an image of a dandelion or a rainbow, below which is written, in cursive font: 'Always Hope.' ('I fucking hate hope,' my friend, who struggled with infertility before having her daughter, told me recently. 'Hope is how you tell women to shut up. Hope is *weaponized*.')

In these spaces where politics are absent, the imperative to be positive and maintain hope is particularly telling of how infertility itself is understood as ultimately mysterious and ephemeral, uprooted from even the medical science on which our outcomes depend. It is standard in many groups, for example, to refer to IVF babies as 'miracles,' or to symbolize babies conceived after miscarriages with rainbows, which invoke the intangible power of hope. Feeling that this imagery erases the difficult, expensive, and very concrete work of infertility, some infertile women on the Infertility subreddit have banned the terms and refer to their children not as 'miracles,' but 'money and science babies.' The shift pokes at the misogyny that shapes women's experiences of infertility from Hannah to the present – how, unlike issues of abortion, consent, employment equality, and so forth, resolving infertility is seen as an issue not of policy or material action, but of passive faith. And it doubles the infertile woman's isolation: in the language of hope, infertility is not a matter between women and the world, but one woman and fate.

Hannah's prayer is recited frequently at Christian infertility groups, where her submission to God's will is held up as a model of faith. 'Some couples see infertility as a malady and become consumed with it,' advises one Christian infertility site:

> They may have uncomfortable feelings toward those who are blessed with children. They may find fault with each

other or become angry with themselves. They may doubt God's wisdom as it applies to their lives ... So what do infertile couples do in the meantime – be happy while everyone else takes their children for picnics in the park? Absolutely! Yes! And may God grant such couples the patience to make their smiles genuine and sincere ... And they can be happy, knowing that God also has a plan for their lives as well. Satisfaction and contentment with one's station in life is always God-pleasing.

If the barren she-monsters of pagan mythology and world folklore are actors, avenging their infertility through acts of evil and destruction, Hannah is redeemed by her passivity and acceptance of a divine plan. In her, we see the origin of the contemporary myth identified by feminist historian Naomi Pfeffer: prior to the development of high-tech reproductive medicine, 'involuntary childless women either suffered their fate in stoic silence, or resolved their childlessness by adoption.' Hannah's response is almost a parody of appropriate feminine submission: she prays silently, denies herself food and drink, and submits immediately to the orders of the male priest who is her only human counsel. It's as she is trying to redeem her deviance, her failure as a woman, by doubling down on femininity, emphasizing her submissiveness and obedience to male authority. When God eventually 'opens her womb,' it's partly in response to her prayer, but also to reward her for her feminine virtue. Because she is pitied, not feared, we know Hannah is not a monster.

Many anthropologists have explained the common fear of infertile women, and history's tendency to demonize, pathologize, and criminalize barren women as more or less evolutionary:

barrenness threatens the continuation of the species. But human extinction is a universal dilemma, and the fact is, the monstrosity of barrenness is still depicted as female. Our ideas about infertility germinated in patriarchy, which is organized around the gender-essentialist idea that women can be reduced to our wombs, and our virtue measured by their function. In cultures that define women as primarily child-bearers and mothers, barren women are scary because we undermine the basis of gendered life.

Woman-as-womb: it sounds comically reductive, a conceptual synecdoche too narrow for anyone living in 2019 to possibly buy into, but I've never met an infertile woman who hasn't expressed some anxiety around feeling less than female because of her condition. Feeling like 'less than a woman' is also a common theme in online support groups; after IVF and isolation, it's one of the most popular topics. ('I feel like a freak and a waste of womanhood,' one writes. Another: 'I am a baby-less monster.') Many women, raised to reject the essentialist idea of women-as-wombs, are as distressed by the antifeminism these feelings imply as they are by the feelings themselves. 'Let me just say that I'm not implying anyone who is child free by choice or cannot get pregnant for one reason or another is any less than a woman,' writes one poster on Reddit:

> I guess what I'm feeling is the counterpart to a man feeling emasculated? And I know that sounds so ridiculous, so please don't judge me. I'm here because I'm ashamed of these feelings. I just … don't feel like a proper woman. I don't feel like a good wife. I don't feel like a good partner … I'm just feeling a huge blow to my ego and identity that I can't really justify, but there you have it.

But the frequency of these feelings of defeminization among infertile women suggests that, in fact, the old idea of woman-as-womb still has some hold on us. Our culture is one where essentialist ideas about women are nominally rejected but still infest daily life, from Facebook memes asserting 'childbirth is women's power' (slash, breastfeeding is; slash, baby-wearing; slash, staying at home; ad nauseam) to Hillary Clinton's insistence that the most important job she has is that of mother and grandmother. If 'woman' is defined by her capacity to bear and mother children, what does it mean that some women can't do this? Are they less female? If not, then maybe we've gotten the definition wrong. Maybe women aren't defined by a working womb. But if wombs don't make a woman, what does? Does any single thing define a woman? And if not, does 'woman,' as a class, make any sense at all? And crucially, if it doesn't, what is a man?

In this way, female infertility asks the key feminist question: what is a woman?

Simone de Beauvoir famously addressed the question in *The Second Sex*, where she theorized woman as 'Other': the constructed object against which man measures and defines himself, and through which he justifies his social and political power. The Other occasions the feminine ideal of the 'eternal feminine' – the enduring cultural myth that the woman is essentially passive, an 'erotic, birthing or nurturing body.' In practice, this confines women to the 'immanent' – the inner, limited worlds of domesticity, bodily concerns, and (of course) reproduction: 'her grasp upon the world is less extended than man's, and she is more closely enslaved to the species.' Men, on the other hand, are 'transcendent': oriented away from themselves, toward the spheres of politics, religion, art, and production.

Yet, as this is an 'artificial product' – not woman's 'true nature in itself, but as man defines her' – the construct of the eternal feminine is forever haunted – taunted, in fact – by its shadow figure, which takes the form of the defiant, aberrant, and devouring female: 'If … woman evades the rules of society, she returns to Nature and to the demon, she looses uncontrollable and evil forces in the collective midst.' The edict of patriarchy is thus to enforce women's adherence to the feminine ideal of immanence, through proscribing 'legitimate marriage and the wish to have children…to strengthen the idea figure of the Mother who will be concerned with the welfare of the next generation.'

De Beauvoir had little to say about infertility, but it's easy to see how barrenness fits into her schema. Infertility is a direct defilement of the patriarchal proposition that women are to 'bear fruit'; all childless women, in some sense, join the other archetypal 'bad women' of history: the lesbian, the prostitute, and the criminal (all of which she describes). More strikingly, we can see in the twin premodern figures of the barren woman, Abyzou and Hannah, interesting examples of the threat the destructive, defiant female poses to the eternal feminine. An infertile woman is not much of a woman, not only because she's barren, but because she's potentially angry, and anger in a woman is irrational, dangerous, and destructive. Chaotic, destructive, and, above all, *active*, Abyzou represents the danger of infertility to patriarchal order, rendering the woman less-than-female, and thus – because woman is the Other against which man defines himself – rendering masculinity suspect in the process. *Calling into question the basis of patriarchy*. A feminist sex worker once told me that society fears the prostitute because she makes visible the lie that is capitalism; in a similar way, I think, the infertile woman makes visible the lie of gender essentialism. That is quite a feat. *Infertility has a lot of power.*

I've wondered about why I never felt compelled to embrace the idea of myself as a monster – in feminist language, reclaim it. I could do this, I could wear my barrenness proudly; I could delight in the fact that my existence is the ultimate rebuke to patriarchal order.

From Lilith Fair to Tumblr posts about witchcraft as a form of self-care, Gen X and millennial women have aligned themselves with the demonic, devouring female archetypes of deep patriarchy. I could do something like this: align myself with Abyzou; write a play about Ursulina de Jesus. But I don't; none of us do. It would require getting angry, for one, and the fact is, however difficult it is to accept anger and defiance in a regular woman, it's impossible to accept it in an infertile one. The bad women of history, the prostitutes and lesbians and childless warriors that feminists like to reclaim, were destructive, but they were destructive toward men. But in the demonology of barrenness, infertile women are angry and destructive toward other women and, not infrequently, children. Monsters like Abyzou, who torture and kill other women at their most vulnerable, are just difficult to square with the third-wave project of reappropriation.

This idea, that anger and bitterness is particularly unacceptable in infertile women, runs through all conversation on infertility, from the Christian prayer groups to my online support groups, where all expressions of 'negativity' are discouraged. When I searched the boards for posts about anger, there were more than a few – 'Warning: Angry Rant!'; 'Angry at My Pregnant Friend'; and so forth – but the stories that followed were riddled with disclaimers and apologies ('I know this sounds bitchy, but'; 'I don't normally act this way and I do love my friend, but'). And on closer inspection, these women didn't seem angry so much as envious or lonely or hurt. Most of the anecdotes were about someone slighting or insulting the infertile woman, after which she felt appalled but refrained from doing anything rash like talk back, or yell, or publicly break down. If she did feel rage, it was expressed later, in the private, anonymous space of the support group. Invariably, the other posters met this with empathy ('I feel this! Let it out, girl!'), but also with encouragements to stay positive and hopeful ('Never give up on your dream. One day you'll say, it was all worth it!'). Faced with the temptation to be vengeful and destructive, infertile women instead become Hannahs: silent, trying to stay positive and faithful, whether in God or fate or the power of our surgeons and doctors.

Two

Society's anxieties about women's progress have always been linked to our anxieties about female infertility. For all the current talk of the epidemic of infertility – backed by a phalanx of medical studies and expert-spouted stats – it's easy to miss that entertainment and news media have been telling us the exact same thing for decades, and that this alarm has moved in lockstep with larger cultural distress over the rising status of women. As Susan Faludi noted in her 1991 classic *Backlash: The Undeclared War Against American Women*, alarm about a disastrous rise in women's infertility was a central trope in the antifeminist discourse of the Reagan era. As women gained civil and social rights, and made gains toward representation in the workplace, lawmakers, media, and the medical industry countered with consistent warnings of an epidemic of feminine loneliness that would leave professional women dissatisfied, isolated, and, most distressingly of all, childless. 'This bulletin of despair is posted everywhere,' Faludi wrote:

> At the newsstand, on the TV set, at the movies, in advertisements and doctors' offices and academic journals. Professional women are suffering 'burnout' and succumbing to an 'infertility epidemic.' Single women are grieving

from a 'man shortage.' The *New York Times* reports: Child-less women are 'depressed and confused' and their ranks are swelling. *Newsweek* says: Unwed women are 'hyster-ical' and crumbling under a 'profound crisis of confidence.' The underlying message, she explains, is that feminism has failed women: 'It must be all that equality that's causing all that pain ... They have gained control of their fertility, only to destroy it.

Throughout the 1980s and 1990s, as American feminist groups lobbied for the always-tenuous rights to legal abortion, birth control, and no-fault divorce, as well as access to equal pay in male-dominated professions, popular culture exploded with cinematic representations of murderous women whose disinterest in – or outright hatred of – the trappings of domes-tic wife-and-motherhood were symptoms of their villainy. Catherine Tramell in *Basic Instinct* ('I hate rug rats'), Annie Wilkes in *Misery* (a former nurse who had murdered infants), and Hedy Carlson in *Single White Female* (a – gasp! – lesbian) reimagined the Victorian femme-fatale archetype for the 1990s. Not only were these women sexually desirous and single, but they were financially independent and, thanks to feminism, socially empowered. Their target was not only the masculine agency of individual men, but the very integrity of the American nuclear family.

While these mainstream, antifeminist thrillers linked a missing maternal instinct to female predation, an interesting subset of horror took a slightly different approach, creating a new class of female villains who were vengeful *because they were infertile*. The most acclaimed chapter in Faludi's *Backlash* analyzed 1987's *Fatal Attraction* as the ultimate expression of Reagan-era Hollywood misogyny. (Director Adrian Lyne on unmarried, childless women: 'It's kind of unattractive, however liberated and emancipated it is. It kind of fights the whole wife role, the whole child-bearing role. Sure, you got your career and your success, but you are not fulfilled as a woman.') A little-discussed feature of villainess Alex Forrest, however, is that she presumed herself infertile after having suffered a traumatic miscarriage. This previous trauma, combined with her age, motivates Alex to reject her married lover's offer to pay for an abortion and sets off the gruesome sequence of events that culminates in her murder.

The 1992 film *The Hand That Rocks the Cradle* repeated this theme of the vengeful, barren woman who threatens the institution of the American family. As her preferred form of address implies, Mrs. Mott is not a career woman, but rather a pregnant stay-at-home wife. When Mrs. Mott's physician husband is accused of sexually assaulting his female patients, he commits suicide; the resulting shock causes Mrs. Mott to miscarry and she is given an emergency hysterectomy. Widowed, childless, and barren, she, like Alex, goes into full revenge mode, posing as a nanny named Peyton to Claire, one of her late husband's accusers. Bereaved of her own family, and incapable of gestating a child, 'Peyton' attempts to poach her rival's. She nurses Claire's infant son so that he prefers her milk over his mother's, frames Claire's husband for an affair that alienates him from his wife's affections, and, eventually, sets up a trap to murder Claire and have it look like an accidental death. Of course, Mrs. Mott dies instead, and order is restored, with a happy family scene that mirrors the conclusion of *Fatal Attraction*: the natural heterosexual unit reunited, newly grateful for its safety and mutual devotion.

While Mrs. Mott is not explicitly coded as feminist – in fact, it is Claire, the sexual assault victim who publicly names and shames her violator, who is the closest thing to a feminist figure in the film – her aggression, wiliness, and dogged entitlement link her to Alex, as well as to the other, more ambiguously barren, villainesses of the era. She's a crazy bitch, and crazy bitches of the 1980s and 1990s always had a whiff of the feminist about them. What she and Alex make explicit, however, is how deeply these qualities were tied to barrenness in the popular imagination, how threatening childless-but-child-wanting women seemed to the American institution of the nuclear family. The fact that both characters suffer miscarriages is no coincidence; the implication is that, even prior to their criminal deeds, they were failed women. In the barren-woman horror of the 1980s and 1990s, failed women are punished twice: once by their bodies and, finally, by the social order they threaten.

While the murderous, childless career lady hadn't quite disappeared by the 2000s – sensationalist media maintained a fixation on barren babynappers – the popular culture of the Bush and Obama eras seemed to soften its condemnation of infertile women. With affirmative action in its second decade, more women than men earning college degrees, and ever-rising numbers of women in white-collar positions of power, the accomplished career woman was no longer a threat but an intractable fact of Western life. At the same time, advances in fertility treatments, including IVF, sperm and egg donation, surrogacy, and egg freezing had expanded options for many women to treat existing infertility conditions and/or postpone starting families (crucially, it also enabled lesbian, queer, and single women to embark on planned family-building at unprecedented rates). News of these innovations, all of which removed reproduction from its 'natural' origin in the heterosexual marriage bed, reached the public (as it still does, frankly) in the language of apocalypse and dystopia: headlines boasted of the 'Wild West' of fertility science, the 'science-fiction' future of reproduction, while op-ed after op-ed mused about the 'social consequences' of babies born via fertility medicine. In other words, concern had shifted from the career woman's barrenness to the fact that she might actually be able to resolve it.

Enter a new stereotype, as Belle Boggs identifies in *The Art of Waiting: On Fertility, Medicine, and Motherhood*: 'the desperate, uptight woman who blindly pursues conception at all costs, destroying her relationships and her dignity in the process.' The advent of the opportunity to pursue conception on her own (i.e., not via the theft of others' husbands or babies) made antifeminist discourse reconceptualize the barren career woman less as a threat to society and more as a threat to herself – often humiliatingly, comically so. If in the 1980s and 1990s, the infertile woman was a monster, in the 2000s, she was a loser.

No one has done more with the trope of the infertile female loser than Tina Fey. She has been working and reworking jokes on the theme of declining female fertility ever since her early-2000s tenure on *Saturday Night Live*'s news-satire segment, Weekend Update, when she was widely heralded as a bold new voice for feminism. Reporting on the wave of alarmist media urging women to start child-bearing in their twenties – lest they find themselves unable to conceive at all – Fey offered what initially seemed like a refreshingly honest critique of the antifeminist message behind these stories:

> According to author Sylvia Hewlett, career women should-
> n't wait to have babies because our fertility takes a steep

drop-off after age 27. And Sylvia's right; I *definitely* should have had a baby when I was 27, living in Chicago over a biker bar, pulling down a cool $12,000 a year. That would have worked out great. But Sylvia's message is basically that feminism can't change nature – which is true, alright. If feminism could change nature, Ruth Bader Ginsberg would be all oiled up on the cover of *Mac* – but she's not.

Her conclusion, spoken to the applause of the audience (which presumably contained a number of career women also exhausted by the media fixation on their declining fertility), was that if she had to choose between her career and a family at this point, she'd choose her career, and take her chances trying to conceive later in life. The following punchline, however, was delivered in a different, much less you-go-girl register: 'And I don't think I could do fertility drugs, because, to me, six half-pound translucent babies is not a miracle. It's gross. I'd rather adopt a baby, I don't need a kid that looks like me. I was an ugly kid.'

In Fey's initial assessment, it's normal – even feminist – for a woman to want both a career and a family, and even to feel anxiety over this pressure. But women who try to 'defy nature' to have children remain unacceptable (recalling the theme of the barren-woman horror movies of the Reagan era), even within an ostensibly feminist framework. What's interesting is less that Fey upholds the ethos of *Fatal Attraction* and *The Hand That Rocks the Cradle*, which coded the infertile career woman as feminist and then punished her for it, but the ways in which she reworks the punishment as an internalized process of deserved self-loathing and shame.

In the ninth episode of the first season of *30 Rock*, Fey devotes a storyline to Liz Lemon's sudden desire for a baby, a type of 'baby craziness' that comes over her like a flu and drives the fast-paced hijinks to come. Here, the central feminist conflict of career vs. kids is played not for horror or shock but for laughs; if Alex Forrest was the Childless Woman as Feminist Monster, the neurotic, self-deprecating Liz is Childless Woman as Buffoon.

Here is Liz talking to Cerie, the young intern who serves throughout the series as the avatar of her insecurities, after the latter has announced her engagement:

> Cerie: We both want to have babies while it's still cool.
> Liz: There's no big hurry to have babies. There are other things in life, like having a career and working and having a job and working.
> Cerie: You can have a career any time. But you only have a really short time when you can be a young, hot mom. If you wait too long, you can be, like, fifty at your kid's graduation.

Later, Liz gives more sincere voice to her ambivalence: 'I worry that I've waited too long. What if my junk goes bad?... My body is telling me something. But my body isn't the boss of me. My brain is.'

But by ignoring her body's urgings, Liz throws the already-disorganized atmosphere at her tv workplace into complete chaos. She screams about sperm donors to a mostly unwitting cast and crew; her boss, Jack Donaghy, lectures her privately for the outburst ('I knew I shouldn't have mentored a woman'); and eventually, through the rapid sequence of half-blunders that typify Fey's comic plotting, Liz, dissociated in a deep hormonal trance, picks up a co-worker's baby and takes it home.

'I don't know what happened!' she gasps. 'One moment I was holding the baby, and the next it was like highway hypnosis, where you are pulling into your driveway but you don't remember driving home.'

While Alex Forrest is a threat to the family, to domestic American life, Liz's threat is less urgent and more contained: despite her professional capabilities and seniority, her 'baby fever' threatens the function of the corporate workplace and the surrogate family she manages there. But more crucially, she is a threat to herself, to the competent, dignified, sane self she has crafted through her education and professionalism. Fey offers up baby-crazy Liz not quite as a cautionary tale; we are meant to side with her, to sympathize. And, unlike Alex, she is allowed redemption. Her baby fever abates once she has reconciled her maternal longing with her intellectual (read: feminist) self-control. The episode concludes with her explaining to Jack that she has realized that she needs to work on herself, and that her 'brain' is not always in charge of her 'body.' Liz's maternal longing becomes, along with her other somatic urges – food, napping, comfortable clothes – another thing the character can joke about, a form of self-deprecation that serves to humble her otherwise wildly successful, aspirational character. Liz's baby craziness doesn't make her a monster, but it does cut her down to size. She is a softened example of the meme Faludi identified over a decade earlier: 'Women who resist baby fever, by controlling their fertility or postponing motherhood, are sh/amed and penalized.'

'Maybe it's impossible to have it all,' Liz explains to Donaghy in the last few seconds of the episode. She sounds like her old self, capable and sane. She steps onto an elevator, intending to head to her office upstairs. 'The career and the family. But if anyone can figure out how to do it, it's me.' We then see that the elevator is going down.

To be fair, there are few ways to write an unproblematic story about a woman under the spell of her 'biological clock.'

Gabrielle Moss, writing in a 2016 piece for *Bustle*, explores how the concept of a 'sudden, helpless onset of biologically-induced baby lust' is, in fact, a debunked piece of pseudoscience, 'introduced to the general public at the same time as in vitro fertilization (IVF) was becoming publicly available.' That is, while there is a limited time frame in which women are able to conceive (magazine articles about this phenomenon always helpfully include a stock image of an egg timer), and there are indeed women who desperately, sincerely *want* to, the idea that such desire is hormonally induced by the aging body is unsupported and even contradicted by scientific research. The myth persists, as Moss points out, because our culture and our economy remain invested in the idea of motherhood as a biological imperative, rather than an active choice:

> We want women to be 'swept up in the urge' to become a mother, rather than making a conscious decision to have a child, because it allows us to keep treating mothers as second-class citizens. A culture that treats motherhood as a kooky whim that overwhelms our dumb lady-brains can keep refusing to give mothers paid parental leave, or force them to work job schedules that keep them from being able to take care of their children (or chase them out of the work force entirely) – because, hey, if you didn't want to be treated like this, you shouldn't have upended your life over a whim, you sillybilly!

Apropos, the feminist woman who does makes a 'conscious choice to have a child' is as derided as her baby-crazy sister in the pop culture of this century's first decade. Three years after she had Liz Lemon stealing an infant in *30 Rock*, Fey returned to the theme of the childless, aging female professional in the surrogacy caper *Baby Mama*. Here, Fey plays Kate, another exaggerated stereotype of the successful single woman who wants a baby. Kate is a sharpened parody of the upper-class, childless urban professional, her characterization honed to communicate the clueless and vaguely colonial privilege of this type (she is the VP of a Whole Foods–type retail enterprise, complete with a grey-ponytailed, spiritual-journeying-with-Native-Americans CEO; her apartment features a reclaimed barnwood coffee table, framed Suzani textiles, and a suspiciously solicitous black doorman who alternately spouts rap lyrics and sage life advice). 'I made a choice,' Kate voices over the opening credits. 'Some women got pregnant; I got promotions.' Cue the montage of consequences: Kate in a goo-eyed trance, intercut with close-up after close-up of cooing white babies: in line at the (presumably fair-trade and organic) café, at the yoga studio, and – disturbingly – arrayed around the conference table at a work meeting she is commandeering. So fixated is she on her childlessness, Kate has reimagined her male employees into the cherubic objects of her desire.

In contrast to Liz, Kate is not under the irrational spell of her biological clock; her decision to become a mother is presented as thought through, rational, and self-justified (she has already planned her maternity leave and the nanny for when she returns to work). But also unlike Liz, Kate is infertile, diagnosed as having a 'one-in-a-million' shot at natural conception due to a T-shaped uterus.[1] To have a biological child, Kate will have to do something 'extreme': surrogacy. The movie's attitude toward this newer infertility technology is established off the bat: when her sister suggests it, Kate immediately replies, 'No, it's weird, it's for weirdos.' But one sweet-smelling-baby-head-in-an-elevator later, and Kate is meeting with a surrogacy agent, nodding along as Chaffee Bicknell, a serene mercenary played by Sigourney Weaver, describes surrogacy to her in the language of self-care-via-capitalism that characterizes Kate's type of Lean-In feminism ('It's just outsourcing,' 'Everyone deserves to be a mother,' etc.). Reconciled to the idea of another woman carrying her baby, Kate begins a romp-filled gestation adventure with Angie, a working-class woman who, in a variation on the Manic Pixie Dream Girl trope, opens Kate's eyes to the impulsive joys foreclosed by her starchy career-gal lifestyle: dressing slutty, dancing, shots, and hooking up with the hot guy at the juice bar. After some initial class-based conflict, the two bond and connect. There is a buoyant and pleasantly girl-powery (nearly queer?) vibe to this plot line: as Angie prepares to birth Kate's baby, Kate gives birth to her new self.

For whatever positive vibes *Baby Mama* generates about surrogacy during these scenes, the viewer is quickly returned to the world view Fey presaged when she declared IVF babies 'gross' on *Weekend Update*. Now in a relationship with Rob, the juice guy, Kate decides to break up with him when she discovers his opinion on surrogacy:

> Rob: It's science fictiony. There's so many kids that need
>   to be adopted. These people would pay $50,000 –
> Kate: It's $100,000, actually …
> Rob: – to, quote, 'have your baby custom-carried by a
>   gestation assistant.'
> Kate: It's complicated.
> Rob: It's a lot of rich people getting what they want.

Rob's scepticism, of course, turns out to be justified by the movie's plot: Angie is, in fact, defrauding Kate, passing off her own baby (naturally conceived with her partner) as Kate's, while collecting the promised cheques. Kate's relationships with both Rob and Angie are shattered; she returns to the natural reality of her singledom and her job. The message here is clear: however attractive surrogacy might seem to infertile women, in the end it is, as her first impulse suggested, weird and for weirdos. Kate's defrauding at the hands of Angie and the agency, her upbraiding by Rob, and the loss of the baby she thought was hers are superficially presented with sympathy, but crucially, we see little of Kate's anger (she is allowed exactly two outbursts at Angie, and in both, her cruel words register as bitterness and classist scorn). Nor do we see anything resembling the most natural response to this loss: grief. As she folds and packs baby clothes in her ridiculous rich-lady apartment, in fact, she looks nothing more than resigned. What else should she have expected, for trying to have a baby this way? In the end, though, because Tina Fey is not Adrian Lyne and Kate Holbrook is not Alex Forrest, she gets her kid, the miracle natural pregnancy Hollywood writers bestow on infertile female characters who have learned their lesson about trying to cheat nature and have a baby outside of the paradigm of hetero, unassisted sex.

'Building a family isn't like opening one of your stores,' Kate's sister tells her early on in the film. 'It's not an executive decision. It's real life. It's messy.' In the end, it's Kate's effort and desire – those qualities that serve her so well in the business world – that come under critique. Babies, the film suggests, shouldn't come to women as a result of desire and effort (let alone financial effort) – they should come naturally, and if the character has repented sufficiently, they will. As a nominally feminist film that was reviewed positively by female critics and drew a large female audience, *Baby Mama* exemplifies a shift away from the trope of baby-crazy loserdom in the feminist woman and toward one that vilifies a specific form of feminist agency, of the *woman who demands*. Unlike in *30 Rock*, where Liz's baby craziness led a normally intelligent woman into utter irrationality, it's Kate's pragmatism and entitlement that lead to her failure. Surrogacy – a treatment that serves a large gay population in the real world – is 'unqueered' to symbolize the danger and cynicism of a reproductive future in which infertile women, emboldened by Lean-In-style feminism, feel entitled to have babies on demand, instead of doing what we've always done: *wait for it to just happen*. The reality of infertility, in which pregnancy certainly does not *just happen*, is erased as Kate's feminist agency is restored to its proper sphere, the workplace.

While the dominant image of infertile women in popular culture mirrors characters like Fey's – upper-middle-class professional white women who 'waited too long' – the reality is much more complex. Latinx reproductive-justice blogger and activist Boricua Feminist explains that not only are women of colour, queer women, and poor women affected by infertility just as much as, if not more than, wealthier white women in straight partnerships, but they also face barriers to infertility care that are inextricable from historical oppression. 'Infertility is impacted by issues of race, class, gender, and sexual orientation,' she writes in her blog post 'Infertility is a Reproductive Justice Issue':

> Some insurance companies won't cover assisted reproductive technology (ART) if it is due to 'social infertility' meaning single women and queer couples. If I had fallen in love with a woman, I may have been denied coverage. In addition, studies have shown that there is a 'knowledge gap' for people of color on fertility options. Many non-white racial groups struggle with infertility at high rates without the same access to resources. The group most

likely to access ART are white, educated, wealthy women. After decades of forced sterilizations of women of color, there is no coincidence that the government is not invested in marginalized communities gaining access.

Excluded from the medical discourse on infertility, racialized, poor, and queer women are also left out of the cultural narrative, compounding their isolation. In her book *Misconception: Social Class and Infertility in America*, an important and rare look at the personal experiences of women with infertility, Ann V. Bell explains how poor women and women of colour are erased from the popular conception of female infertility:

> Infertility is stereotypically depicted as a white, wealthy women's issue, shaped by media images of celebrities receiving IVF and reality shows highlighting the lives of families with sets of multiples. But in reality, poor women and women of color have equivalent, if not slightly higher rates of infertility than their wealthier counterparts.

As mainstream attention focuses on upper-class white women's infertility, usually in the context of scientific advances in fertility medicine, it becomes easier than ever for the public to view it not as a general women's health issue, but a type of malaise of the privileged – overlooking the significant experiences of poor women, queer women, and women of colour who are struggling with the same (if not worse) physical and emotional consequences. It also plays directly into racist and classist beliefs, rooted in old-school eugenicist theory, that poor women and non-white women are 'hyperfertile' – unthinking reproducers who are closer to fertile nature than white women and should be encouraged to have fewer, rather than more, children. In sub-Sarahan Africa, where contagious diseases cause as many as one in three women to have second-ary infertility, efforts to introduce programs that would diag-nose and treat women have failed to attract adequate funding, due to the perception that the area is already overpopulated. The situation is not too far from our own: across North Amer-ica, free or low-cost women's health clinics – themselves all too few and far between – will provide birth control, early pregnancy care, and abortion-referral services, but few services for diagnosing and treating infertility.

Without access to private medical and psychological treat-ment, poor women and women of colour report feeling margin-alized in free support groups (such as the online groups I'm in) because of the perception that they should not be having kids in the first place. Their erasure from narratives of infertility is self-reinforcing: because most academic studies on infertility draw data from fertility clinics, which are frequented by the patients who can afford to access them, infertile women who are poor or of colour are typically excluded from research, so that white, upper-middle class women are overrepresented in the academic discussion of infertility as well as the one in popular culture. It also limits much-needed investigations into condi-tions that are specific to marginalized demographics. For exam-ple, the treatment of fertility-impairing fibroids, which black women experience at significantly high rates, and are woefully under-researched compared to conditions more common in white women, such as endometriosis. Psychological and social issues that vary across groups, such as the heightened taboo against seeking help for infertility in some working-class Black communities, also remain neglected. The gap in research allows the stereotyping of these women to go unchallenged, so that in the public narrative of reproduction, poor women and women of colour are only one thing: hyperfertile. And the image of female infertility remains that of a privileged, wealthy white woman who, in the folk tradition, is something of a monster.

The acclaimed Hulu series *The Handmaid's Tale* premiered in spring 2017, a couple months after our surrogate had miscarried our third and sole remaining frozen embryo. I had read Margaret Atwood's original 1985 novel in high school and adored it, relishing the idea of a feminist allegory that imagines a literal patriarchy as a hellish dystopia. But now, pitching around in the dark of my own infertility, and grappling with the complexities of my relationship with our gestational carrier, even watching the trailer for the first season, with its gorgeously wrought images of enslaved women forced to carry the children of abusive women – privileged, white, infertile women *like me* – felt like a type of pointed, personal assault. I posted about it on one of my surrogacy Facebook groups: 'Is anyone able to actually watch this?'

No way, the other intended parents chorused, *I just had a miscarriage, and I know it would be a trigger.* Or, *No thanks, people misunderstand surrogacy already and I don't want to support anything that will lead to more ignorance.* But mostly: *No, I can't bear the idea of seeing more evil infertile women right now, no thanks.*

One woman in the group who had actually watched the series graciously summarized it for me. It's a nightmare scenario in which women lose all their rights because some are infertile; the infertile women are wealthy and sociopathic and beat the surrogates, whom they own as slaves; surrogacy is an evil system that symbolizes the larger evil of the patriarchal dystopia of Gilead.

Based on my memory of the book, I thought maybe her assessment was an exaggeration. But when I was finally able to watch the series – my son safely past the second-trimester mark in the belly of his very willing and proud gestational carrier – I found that this summary had, sadly, been pretty accurate. The enforcers of Gilead are infertile women and men, but the women (called Wives) are much, *much* worse than the men. No militaristic male enforcer in the series – including the machine-gun-equipped Eyes of God who mass-murder dissidents – are as scary as Aunt Lydia, the sadistic handler for Gilead's handmaids (she has their eyes gouged out for insubordination); no wealthy patriarch – including Fred, the titular handmaid's commander and prospective inseminator – is as intimately violent as the Wives, who whip, confine, and starve their handmaids when they fail to conceive. The unique horror of the 'ceremony,' wherein the commander rapes the handmaid with his wife positioned at the head of the bed, is in fact a concession to the Wives, who would otherwise feel threatened by the idea of their men having sex with their fertile slaves. In this patriarchy, the most creative and intimate oppressors are infertile women.

In the critical reviews of the series, Serena Joy, the Wife who gets the most airtime and the mistress of the house where Offred was placed, was lauded as a more complex variation on the villainesses who populate the dystopia. Prior to the Revolution, Serena Joy had been an author, in the antifeminist women's self-help genre; she appeared to enjoy more liberated feminine pleasures such as non-procreative sex and choosing her own fashionable clothing. Her willing transformation to Gilead wife, complete with scripting the legislation that would prevent women from reading and writing, as she once so enjoyed, can be seen as a fraught, and perhaps even understandable, manoeuvre to retain a measure of power in the emerging patriarchal order. But when it comes to her central conflict – her infertility – she remains maddeningly flat, a stereotype of the bitter, jealous barren woman made scarily literal (she beats Offred after each negative pregnancy test). Her infertility is a source of entitlement and constant violence, void of any representation of the grief or even sadness every infertile person knows as its main feature. 'We tried for many, many years,' she explains to Offred in an early episode – but the viewers do not see this trying, nor the agony that Serena Joy must have experienced when all that trying failed. To the infertile viewer, Serena Joy isn't a complex new take on woman as patriarchal collaborator, but an old stereotype of the woman made monstrous by her barrenness.

Grief is most present in Gilead in the lives of the hand-maids, who are separated from their genetic children by the regime. In a hauntingly grotesque scene, handmaiden Ofwar-ren gives birth in the home of her Commander, surrounded by other handmaidens, while the Wife – the legal mother of the child – performs a simulated labour and childbirth supported by other Gilead wives. The unreality of the Wife's labour, performed in the spotless and beautifully appointed parlour, all hushes and whispers, is contrasted pointedly with the handmaid's real labour, amid blood and screaming and healthy gore. As the child is handed off from handmaid to Wife, the camera lingers on Ofwarren, her expression one of relief – for getting through labour, for having produced a healthy child for Gilead – mixed with a heartbreaking, sudden grief that she must now separate from her child. Ofwarren's maternal grief is an ongoing plot in the series; her storyline concludes when she is sentenced to murder for trying to kidnap back her baby. Again, her understandable heartbreak is contrasted with that of the Wife, who keeps the child, a brittle parody of a non-maternal, barren shrew. She handles the baby so roughly it shrieks and she lambastes Ofwarren as ungrateful, calling her 'it.' Whatever suffering the Wife endured before the Revolution due to her infertility is not only erased but called out as somehow false; the narrative only validates the maternal grief of the naturally fertile.

In an interview about the series, Atwood drew parallels between Gilead and our own historical moment, explaining that the worst abuses against women are often committed by other women, à la female voters ushering in the antifeminist Trump and consistently lobbying against reproductive rights legislation across U.S. government. This is true, of course, but it also neglects the way in which these intragender abuses are mediated by race, ability, and sexuality in addition to class. As writer Sherronda J. Brown notes on the blog Afropunk, the premise of *The Handmaid's Tale* is essentially a deracinated version of American slavery, with the young fertile handmaids (in the segregated world of book, they are all white, while in the TV series they include women of colour) standing in for Black American slaves: they are owned and controlled as property, raped, stripped of their names, and publicly lynched for disobedience. The rape and reproductive servitude of the handmaids seems especially modelled on the abuses Black women faced during slavery:

> The systematic sexual and reproductive violences on the show terrify those who view the story as a future dystopian (im)possibility for whiteness, when it is in fact a historical ghost for Black people who were enslaved … [Essentially], *The Handmaid's Tale* depicts cis white women stripped of the ability to bear and nurture one's own children without government interference or barriers created through white supremacy and systemic oppression. This is a position

that they have never seen themselves depicted in, and it terrifies them.

White women, of course, were and are complicit in the systematic racism and sexism that results in the lack of reproductive justice for Black women and other women of colour, just as cisgender women are responsible for the diminished social, medical, and legal opportunities for transgender women. But in Gilead, women oppressing women is just about fertility and class – a curiously flat dynamic that discourages white female viewers from considering not only that, for marginalized women, Gilead has always been close to reality but also, how that's always partly on us.

In Gilead, then, female infertility becomes a stand-in for other markers of privilege: whiteness, wealth, heterosexuality. It's an easy move: media reports of infertility invariably depict barren women as economically privileged and, in sensationalist stories of the new surrogacy and egg-donation industries, the exploiters of poor, often non-white women. It's a misdirect, of course – as many if not more working-class women as upper-class women suffer from infertility and desire access to reproductive technologies, including advanced treatments such as surrogacy. But rather than highlight the unequal circumstances of infertile women, perhaps resulting in increased demand for funded reproductive health care, *The Handmaid's Tale* uses infertility as a cheat, a way to evade a more difficult and complicated conversation about race, gender, and class.

In the misogynist vision of Lyne's *Fatal Attraction*, barrenness stands in for the threat of feminism, the literal vanquishing of the American nuclear family; the infertile woman is a threat to men. In Fey's liberal pop feminism, barrenness symbolizes the folly of an overly rigid feminism that pressures women to sublimate their biological desires and defy nature; the infertile woman is a threat to herself. But *The Handmaid's Tale* was not scripted by a misogynist nor a girl-powery comedian, it was adapted from the work of a legendary feminist novelist. It is, unequivocally, a feminist text. And yet, in its world, female barrenness is not only just as threatening, just as disgusting, just as destructive as it is in these earlier works, it is outright oppressive, a necessary engine for patriarchy itself. There is ambiguity here: from her earliest works, Atwood was a nuanced critic of second-wave radical feminism, particularly of the emphasis on 'natural womanhood' that, in its extreme forms, condemned technological advances such as the birth control pill, gynecology, and IVF as patriarchal intrusions on the female body. Some writers have noted that Gilead is, in fact, a dystopia that combines features from right-wing evangelicalism with propositions from radical feminists such as Andrea Dworkin and Gena Corea; while women are stripped of all civil rights and reproductively enslaved (the nightmare scenario of radical feminism), the regime also eschews all reproductive technology in favour of a mandated 'sisterhood' that venerates women's 'natural' role as reproducers (the all-female, drug-free 'birthing circles' in the series closely mimic the idealized vision of childbirth in the second-wave women's health movement). This complicated vision of patriarchy – in which the rhetoric of radical feminism has been twisted to serve men's interests – elevates *The Handmaid's Tale* above more reductive feminist analyses of misogyny but, ultimately, repeats the misogynistic silence around female infertility present in both right-wing and radical feminist ideologies. There is no question, for example, that Atwood takes an anti-assisted-reproduction stance not only throughout *The Handmaid's Tale* (Gilead's infertility epidemic is due, in part, to a gene-splicing experiment gone awry; the handmaids are but an analog version of high-tech procedures such as IVF), but also in later works such as *Oryx and Crake* (a hellish scenario here is the wholesale techno-engineering of human beings, to be bought and sold as ready-made families to those able to pay). While Atwood was critical of Dworkin et al.'s definition of the 'natural' woman and mother, she ultimately sides with them in her alarmist warnings against a future in which babies can be made not via nature, but via women's will.

Thus, the most openly feminist text of the Trump era is one that betrays infertile women, defining them as not only unworthy of families, but as patriarchal collaborators. In Gilead, the most decisive conflict is not between men and women, but between feminist and antifeminist women, and this dynamic is flattened into a dyad that tracks back to the monsters of antiquity: between women who are fertile and women who are not. There is no way around its central logic: in Gilead, some women are oppressed because others are barren. In *The Handmaid's Tale*, the infertile woman assumes her worst form: she is a threat to other women, and to feminism itself.

Three

Feminism has long been either dismissive of – or outright hostile to – the plight of infertile women. This might surprise most self-identified feminists. Having cut their teeth on the rhetoric of the pro-choice movement, with slogans like 'Every mother a willing mother; every child a wanted child' and 'My body, my choice,' they assume that the logic of reproductive rights goes both ways: if women should have the choice to not be mothers, surely they should have the choice to *be* mothers?

But the roots of the reproductive rights movement are not in choice – at least, not in the universal, expansive way in which modern feminists talk about choice. Rather, early advocates of birth control and abortion in the West were concerned with limiting maternity, especially for poor, disabled, and racialized populations (particularly Black and Indigenous women).

In the early twentieth century, decades after the first watershed feminist texts – Mary Wollstonecraft's *A Vindication of the Rights of Women* and Margaret Fuller's *Woman in the Nineteenth Century* – legal reforms including suffrage, property rights, and access to higher education rolled out across the West, marking the successes of feminism's first wave. New technologies in birth control (first, barrier methods like cervical caps and condoms, and then the first generation of contraceptive pills) and surgical abortion went hand in hand with these social advances, providing a means for women to enjoy their new-found freedom and avoid the drudgery of continuous pregnancy and childbirth that characterized Victorian womanhood.

However, the first-wave feminist project was inextricable from the larger cultural anxiety about the precariousness of race and class in an era marked by mass immigration, incipient civil rights for Black Americans, and the rise of unions. The architects of the early women's rights movement were white and middle- to upper-class, and their achievements were tremendously beneficial to other women of their ilk. Yet working-class women, Black, Latina, and Indigenous women, immigrant women, and disabled women continued to face restrictions from voting, fair wages, and education, as they do to this day. In some aspects, the transformations of the first wave actively harmed them, as was the case with the entry of white women into the professional sphere, which saw them employing Black and Latina women to assume their domestic tasks for below-living-wage labour. It is the great tragedy of feminism that the first critical push for female liberation happened at the expense of the women who were and are the most vulnerable.

The erasure of women of colour from early feminism was repeated in its push for reproductive rights. Margaret Sanger, who started Planned Parenthood, founded birth-control clinics, published pamphlets on sexual education, and lobbied for legislation to make abortion safe and legal during an era when even the idea that women might want to have sex for reasons other than reproduction was blasphemous (indeed, she was jailed over many of these acts). Doubly so when coupled with her plainspoken advocacy for women's equality, which she saw as inextricable from their ability to control reproduction.

'Birth control is ... the first step she must take to be man's equal,' Sanger wrote in 1920. 'It is the first step they must both take toward human emancipation.'

But Sanger's ultimate enthusiasm for contraception was inseparable from a larger conversation about how modern nations might better society through population control. 'If we are to develop in America a new race with a racial soul, we must keep the birth rate within the scope of our ability to understand as well as to educate,' she wrote the same year. 'We must not encourage reproduction beyond our capacity to assimilate our numbers so as to make the coming generation into such physically fit, mentally capable, socially alert individuals as are the ideal of a democracy.' Her statements would later be regarded as foundational in government-sponsored eugenics programs, erected in the U.S. in thirty-three states, which forcibly sterilized at least 65,000 citizens (a large proportion of whom were Black and Indigenous) from the 1900s to the 1970s. (In Canada, a similar program saw the compulsory sterilization of thousands – the majority Indigenous women – up until the 1970s; First Nations women report that coerced sterilizations continue to this day).

In recent years, right-wing anti-choice activists have exploited Sanger's eugenicist connections, citing her work promoting contraception in Black American communities as evidence that she sought to eliminate or reduce the African-American population as a whole. As pro-choice Black feminists have countered, this is a misrepresentation: Sanger likely had no white-supremacist ideals and was a lifelong supporter of civil rights (Martin Luther King, Jr., was a recipient of the Margaret Sanger Award for human rights in 1966 and praised her contributions to the Black community). To be sure, Sanger ushered in formidable change, helping repeal laws preventing the distribution of birth control across the U.S. and accelerating a key shift from Victorian mores to a more sexually permissive society. Still, as reproductive-justice non-profit Trust Black Women has pointed out, Sanger's connection to the architects of 'polite eugenics,' which hinged on an ableist understanding of the genetic inferiority of people with mental and physical disabilities, adds ambiguity to Sanger's story. If she wasn't a genocidal white supremacist, her idea of reproductive rights was still equivocal – certainly, she was selective about which people should have the right to their natural fertility, or to children at all. In her 1934 treatise, 'America Needs a Code for Babies,' she proposed that American couples apply for parenthood licences:

> Article 3. A marriage license shall in itself give husband and wife only the right to a common household and not the right to parenthood.
> Article 4. No woman shall have the legal right to bear a child, and no man shall have the right to become a father, without a permit for parenthood.
> Article 5. Permits for parenthood shall be issued upon application by city, county, or state authorities to married couples, providing they are financially able to support the expected child, have the qualifications needed for proper rearing of the child, have no transmissible diseases, and, on the woman's part, no medical indication that maternity is likely to result in death or permanent injury to health.
> Article 6. No permit for parenthood shall be valid for more than one birth.

In the wake of attacks on Planned Parenthood in the U.S. and abroad, there has been a recent interest on the left in rehabilitating its founder, to claim that she had 'advanced views on race relations' for her time (*Washington Post*) or that instead of advocating 'the process of weeding out the unfit [and] of preventing the birth of defectives' (Sanger's words), she 'thought people should have the children they wanted' (NPR).

England's equivalent to Sanger was Marie Stopes – another firebrand who faced constant censure and opposition for her publications on sex and reproduction (which included some of the first woman-centred discussion of the clitoris, and admonitions against rape within marriage). Stopes is still regarded as a positive figurehead of the British reproductive rights and feminist movements: women's health clinics still bear her name, and her more sanguine quotes about equitable love and marriage regularly appear in GIF form on Tumblr feminist blogs (popular: 'every heart desires a mate'). Yet she fought as tirelessly for the sterilization of mentally and physically disabled people as she did for women's rights to accurate sexual education. In 1920's *Radiant Motherhood: A Book for Those Who Are Creating the Future*, she recommended 'the sterilisation of those totally unfit for parenthood [to be] made an immediate possibility, indeed made compulsory.' Having achieved renown in international eugenics and feminist circles, Stopes attempted in the late 1930s to woo Adolf Hitler into adopting her ideas about 'racial purification' through contraception and sterilization, sending him a book of her poetry with a personal inscription. It was her hope that the führer would distribute her writings on sex and contraception in Germany's women's health clinics. (Hitler shut down these clinics instead.)

Stope's Mothers' Clinic in London, which provided contraception and family-planning advice to thousands of women, opened under the motto 'Every child a wanted child' – a slogan that still shows up on protest signs and abortion-rights blogs to this day. But her politics, like Sanger's, makes it clear just how whopping a misnomer it is. Every child a wanted child … for women we deem worthy of wanting them. Every child a wanted child … for white women, for financially stable women, for able-bodied women who are straight and in heterosexual unions. And what about the women who wanted children but couldn't have them? Early reproductive-rights literature and clinic work rarely, if ever, addressed the issue of infertility in women – in fact, if you went by first-wave feminist activism and writing alone, one would think infertile women did not exist.

This could not have been further from the case. Mainstream journalism, with its focus on IVF clinics and the rich, older white ladies who use them, has disseminated an idea that female infertility is a modern epidemic, a symptom of a generation of career women who have delayed child-bearing until it is too late. But Western scholars and politicians in the late nineteenth and early twentieth century were deeply concerned about what they saw as an unacceptable level of unwanted childlessness in the upper and middle classes – infertility affecting up to one in five couples in some early studies (identical to figures from the most recent surveys). Their concern was largely nationalistic – where will the white race go? what will happen to the upper class? – and deeply misogynistic, fuelled by the Victorian ideal of woman as a 'natural' mother. While Sanger and Stopes were opening their clinics and penning their tracts, the emerging discipline of gynecology was solidifying a discourse of infertility that largely blamed women for a couple's unwanted childlessness. As Naomi Pfeffer describes, the first infertility specialists theorized female infertility as a 'deserved punishment of indiscipline … the price paid by women for slack moral habits.' She continues:

Women who led a worthless life, filled with idleness, sensuality and rich food, were less fertile than hard-working women who ate simple fare. Sexualized and sexually active women – epitomized by prostitutes – who took a great many hot baths, rose at ten or eleven in the morning, and generally led an 'animal life,' rarely had children. A similar fate awaited depressed or melancholy women, those who drank too much alcohol or abused drugs.

Diagnostic and therapeutic techniques for women, including the use of pessaries (a type of suppository) and surgical manipulation of the uterus, were first-line procedures, at the expense of needed research on male sterility and sperm health. This was in line with the androcentric thrust of medicine during the period:

> The male norm was infused with health, whereas women's bodies were defined by their susceptibility to radical instability ... a number of related tendencies contributed to doctors' stubborn adherence to an image of men as robust, and women as inherently unstable and in constant need of medical attention.

Infertile women sought out the new medical treatments, though access was limited for many. Like some other gynecological advances, however, infertility treatment was largely researched on working-class women, who could solve their infertility by volunteering for untested procedures. Oral historian Elizabeth Roberts documented childless women in England in the Edwardian period, noting that while women were 'eager for medical help and assiduously [sought] it out,' only major voluntary hospitals provided free or cheap treatment, excluding rural women who could not access it. Some sterility treatment

was available as part of health-care programs for English workers, but as these workers were men, and the treatments were
to be performed on men, women were left out. Pfeffer writes:
'The view of sterility as a "woman's problem" doubly disadvan-
taged women: not only were they made the focus of any medical
interventions, they were denied access to them when wanted
by virtue of their supposed dependency on their husbands.'

As such, the voices of infertile women in the first-wave
era are silenced twice, first by the reproductive-rights movement's emphasis on limiting women's reproduction rather than
truly freeing them to choose, and again by gynecology, which
objectified and pathologized infertile women even as it sought
to treat them.[2]

It is tempting to wish that the first reproductive-rights
activists had worked with infertile women in establishing
health care for women – if not to provide interventions that
would help them conceive, then at least to document their
experience, register their voices, provide a less misogynistic
context in which they could receive diagnosis and practical
support. There are few more striking examples of the costs of
essentialism (woman is always-already a mother) than the
agony of an infertile woman who has been socially marginalized and privately scorned for her failure. By ignoring these
women, first-wave feminism missed out on this useful avenue
of critique. But it's naive to imagine that this was an oversight
– to take 'Every child a wanted child' at face value. In light of
the eugenicist connections of the movement's key players,
first-wave feminism appears to be less about empowering
women to plan the families they desire than about limiting
maternity, full stop – anti-natalism lite.

Reproductive rights, then as now, were framed around the
negative: the right to not have children, to *not* be pregnant, to

not be a mother. There is good reason for this: even the non-eugenicist birth-control advocates of the movement analyzed motherhood under patriarchy as a burden on individual women and a threat to female advancement as a whole (anarchist Emma Goldman: 'Morality and its victim, the mother – what a terrible picture! Is there indeed anything more terrible, more criminal, than our glorified sacred function of motherhood?'). This anti-maternal bias not only circumscribed the proper subject of feminism as the woman trying to not have kids, but also led to mothers' issues such as custody and child care being put on the back burner for the first years of women's activism. It's not surprising that infertile women aren't included in first-wave feminism: within its world view, their desires are not only unimportant, they are invalid.

By the 1980s, the feminist movement had become highly organized and fractured, and along with it, feminist views on infertility. Mainstream women's rights activism, of which reproductive-care clinics like Sanger's remained central, built on the work of first-wave feminists in continuing to push for legal changes to ensure widespread access to contraception, abortion, and sexual health education, and to combat systemic abuses such as violence against women, workplace inequity, and marriage laws that disfavoured women. While the eugenics of the early twentieth century were gone, replaced with a (very) nominal inclusion of poor women and women of colour and an emphasis on 'choice' and 'rights' – no one was calling for sterilizing disabled women, or requiring licences for prospective parents – infertility remained an orphan issue. While some mothers' issues were included on the list of central thinkers and activists, an idea of motherhood as conscription into patriarchy remained central to feminist theory and action. In her cornerstone 1962 book, *The Feminine Mystique*, Betty

Friedan, an American mother of three children, decried how masculine rule submitted women to the drudgery and triviality of mothers' work 'in lieu of more meaningful goals' – the fulfillment of professional work outside the home that was traditionally done by men. Feminist organizing still circulated around the same figure: white, middle-class, able-bodied, and in need of birth control and abortion services. Planned Parenthood did not include infertility workups in its list of services, for example, and, as far as I know, the National Organization for Women never released a policy statement on researching or treating female infertility. 'Every child a wanted child' was still an exclusive mandate, assuming that every woman who wanted a child was capable of having one.

The rhetoric of 'choice' is especially weak in addressing the histories and needs of women of colour. For Black, Latinx and Indigenous women in the West, reproductive 'choice' had always been circumscribed by more than abortion and birth-control law. How women of colour had and raised children was also a matter of wide-ranging systemic policy and conventions. For example, the forced-sterilization policies of the early and mid-twentieth centuries, unequal child welfare practices that removed children from homes without parental consent, racist policing and incarceration policies that separate families of colour, and lack of access to general health care that still results in higher maternal morbidity for Black women.

In the 1990s, Black feminist activists working with a group named SisterSong expressed dissatisfaction with the reproductive-rights movement and defined a more holistic, intersectional framework: reproductive justice. 'Every woman has the right to decide if and when she will have a baby,' writes feminist blogger Angi Becker Stevens. She also has the right 'to decide if she will not have a baby, and to parent the children she already has in a safe environment and healthy community, without the threat of either interpersonal or state violence.' The broad approach of reproductive justice, while focused on the lived realities of women of colour, goes beyond the nega-tive-rights rhetoric of the mainstream pro-choice movement to affirm the right of women to have children if they so desire – and opens the possibility for a feminist, intersectional under-standing of female infertility. With its emphasis on equal access to care, it allows us to consider that barriers to infertility care and treatment, including ART, are in fact deeply raced and classed violations of women's rights. However, as with much of the work done by feminists of colour, the reproductive-justice movement was marginalized within the mainstream feminist movement, and the popular rhetoric around women's reproduction remained that of the liberal 'pro-choice' sort. As a result, little theoretical room existed to discuss the concerns of women who wanted to have children but could not.

This is not to say infertile women were invisible during this period. We were not. The 1980s and 1990s saw the creation of a multi-million-dollar, booming industry around new reproductive technologies that purported to solve female infertility – as much a problem in the late twentieth century as ever. While mainstream liberal feminists continued to focus their reproductive activism on birth control and abortion, radi-cal, socialist, and eco-feminist activists of the second wave turned their attention to these new technologies: IVF, artificial insemination, egg and sperm donation, and surrogacy. These feminists departed from their liberal sisters in their deep distrust of the narrative of 'progress' espoused by the first wave; they aimed not for 'equality' of men and women, but for the validation and liberation of women as a separate and distinct class. A big part of this involved moving away from the disdain first-wave and mainstream feminists had for pregnancy and motherhood – to, as recommended by American feminist poet Adrienne Rich, rediscover and thus reclaim the natural power of maternity, on women's own terms. There were outliers – Canadian-American radical feminist Shulamith Firestone imagined a utopia in which machines conceive and birth babies, freeing up women to do the imaginative and transcendent work previously limited to men; American *SCUM Manifesto* author Valerie Solanas hoped that genetic technologies would eventually prevent women from having to breed with men altogether, a transformation that would ultimately eliminate the male sex – but most radical and eco-feminists had a deep distrust of medical and technological intervention in the female body. This led to one of the stranger episodes in the history of the women's movement, which saw the most radical cohorts of feminists actively lobbying against the expressed interests of infertile women.

Behold the first meeting of FINRRAGE, the Feminist International Network of Resistance to Reproductive and Genetic Engineering, which grew out of a smaller, more loosely organized group called FINNRET (Feminist International Network on New Reproductive Technologies): in the rural setting of Comilla, Bangladesh, 145 women from thirty-five countries structured meetings around the grassroots, knowledge-sharing traditions of the feminist second wave. An inaugural ceremony featured a traditional Filipino hand-clapping ceremony to build solidarity, two Indian activists showering the crowd with flowers, and a group of Nepalese women performing a folk song devoted to the struggles of working women in their home country. In discussions, women shared their concerns as lawyers, health workers, teachers, scientists, labour activists, environmentalists, and academics. The display of cultural and professional diversity only underscored the unity of their beliefs, which centred on the medical and social dangers posed by reproductive technologies – including then-new forms of hormonal birth control like Depo-Provera, genetic testing of fetuses, and experimental 'fertility vaccines' – posed to women and children, particularly in the Global South. 'It became clear that the rationale behind [these technologies] is the control of women's reproduction, and that [they] use women as experimental subjects,' recalled one participant after the conference. 'Ironically, pro-fertility technologies such as IVF have now spread to countries such as India, which for decades has been implementing coercive population control methods.' When it came to the infertile women who ostensibly motivated the development of IVF and who were, in fact, the driving market for the technology, the committee's consensus zeroed in on issues of control: the technology was ineffective and often dangerous, making it tantamount to medical experimentation; it represented an incursion into the female body by male-designed, techno-medical powers; and its unfettered growth shifted attention away from more sustainable solutions to female infertility, such as preventing sexually transmitted diseases or workplace exposure to fertility-damaging chemicals. In the words of the same FINRRAGE participant, '[IVF] keeps offering solutions to the problem of infertility that are harmful for women's health and invading upon the women's body without finding the causes of infertility.'

They were not totally wrong. At the time, IVF failed to produce a child more often than it succeeded; while the technology has improved tremendously, more IVF cycles still fail than not. Then more than now, but still, the side effects of IVF medication and its related surgeries can be not only dangerous, but, in some cases, lethal. But women still wanted it, which required FINRRAGE feminists to rely on a lot of philo-sophical sleight-of-hand. Faced with the idea that women might *choose* this technology – or that it very much helped the women that it did work for – they dismissed women's agency out of hand. In contrast to the choice-based liberal feminism that had come to dominate the public discussion around contraception and abortion, the FINRRAGE participants shared a skepticism about the validity of women's 'choices' under patriarchal capitalism. As American abortion historian Rosalind Pollack Petchesky had put it, 'The "right to choose" means very little when women are powerless … [W]omen make their own reproductive choices, but they do not make them just as they please; they do not make them under condi-tions that they themselves create but under social conditions and constraints which they, as mere individuals, are powerless to change.' In the case of infertility, these social constraints included the tremendous pressure to reproduce for white, middle-to-upper-class Western women and the still-all-potent link between a woman's worth and her status as a mother. (A persistent theme in anti-reproductive-technology feminist writing is that increasing women's access to reproductive tech-nology enshrines the cultural prerogative for women to breed, by allowing them to take extreme physical and psychological risks to have a child.)

The Comilla meeting of FINRRAGE, while not widely known to the public, nonetheless allowed the first major femi-nist perspective on infertility, and on the infertile woman, to cohere and take root in the women's movement. FINRRAGE members included American feminist and academic Janice Raymond, who went on to author the anti-reprotech tome *Women as Wombs*; Gena Corea, whose 1987 *The Mother Machine* is often called 'the bible' of FINRRAGE; Maria Mies,

the German sociologist whose ecocentric approach to reproductive technology went on to inform the technophobic wing
of modern eco-feminism; and Australian biologist Renate
Klein, who became radical feminism's most vocal opponent
of surrogacy and the 'abortion pill' RU486. While the FINRRAGE
recommendations were never directly implemented, the canon
they inspired went on to inform legislation that banned surrogacy in several European countries and informed various
facets of IVF regulation in Australia. In Canada, a two-volume
collection of feminist anti-reprotech essays called *Misconceptions* provided an oft-cited counterpoint to policies that
increased (some) access to IVF, sperm, and donor gametes;
one can get the gist from this quote by Canadian writer and
documentarian Gwynne Basen, who imagines the future
thoughts of a person conceived through IVF: 'My parents
aren't my parents. My mother is a virgin. My father is a
powerful magician. You can buy babies from a store. I am not
the results of anyone else's sexual act.'

As extreme as it may sound, the thinking of radical feminists on technology appealed to a romanticized nature, and a
monolithic view of patriarchy, that was in line with many
areas of academic and popular feminism. Despite the later
forays of FINRRAGE-aligned feminists such as Raymond and
Germaine Greer into institutionalized transphobia, the most
powerful of these radical feminists held university posts in
women's studies departments and are still routinely cited in
both academic writing and mainstream articles on the topic of
reproductive technology and, by extension, the infertile people
who use it. Their ideas got a lot of play in the women's health
movement of the 1980s, which was responsible for re-normal-
izing midwifery and natural childbirth as well as non-medical
alternatives to birth control such as ovulation charting; the

contemporaneous versions of *Our Bodies, Ourselves* devoted a chapter to the dangers of reproductive technology, with only a paragraph or so on the actual experience of infertility.

In this way, technophobic radical feminism stood in stark opposition to the liberal feminist idea of 'reproductive rights.' While liberal feminists – their rhetoric of choice so compatible with consumer capitalism, and thus the dominant strand of feminist thought at the time – had framed abortion and birth-control access as a matter of individual liberty, and held that a pro-woman society was one in which women could exercise this choice, feminists such as Raymond and Klein felt that legislation around women's family-building should reflect the social good of women as a whole. In the romantic world view of 1980s radical feminism, a good female body is one free of the technological interference of patriarchal medicine, untainted by chemicals, and unaltered by drugs and surgeries, but also by the imposition of unwanted pregnancy. The seeming incompatibility of allowing access to abortion while restricting access to technologies like IVF was justified by appealing to the larger female good. Mainstream liberal feminism might support women seeking access to reproductive technology theoretically – and voice this when pressed – but, in keeping with its legacy in the early work of Sanger et al., it remained tightly focused on the rights of women to not have children. So the established canon of feminist literature on infertility remains largely radical-feminist: wary of technology, romantic about nature, and critical of the liberal-feminist idea of choice.

Over two decades later, few people outside of religious circles view most reproductive technologies, like IVF and ovulation stimulation, as controversial. Outcomes have improved tremendously since the early days of fertility medicine, and the nightmare scenario envisioned by Basen, in which the children of IVF are emotionally or physically harmed by their conception, did not come to pass. (Louise Brown, the first child conceived by IVF, recently celebrated her fortieth birthday with a social media tribute to her mother and the doctors who developed the technology that helped bring her into the world.) To be sure, there are some holdovers: Germaine Greer is still around, writing weird shit about fertility treatments being tools of patriarchy when she is not deriding transgender women. (In this strand of radical feminism, the female reproductive system is the root of feminine identity; having a dysfunctional one, or lacking one altogether, both infertile women and trans women are suspect at best.) There are Twitter accounts booping out stories of the 'untold victims IVF,' and quotes by Corea sometimes flit by on my feminist Facebook feeds.

But by and large, feminist discourse on reproductive technology has turned away from the horrors of IVF to refocus on the complex, ever-changing, and potentially harmful practices of egg and sperm donation and surrogacy, or third-party reproduction. This skepticism of 3PR is grounded in a radical feminist critique of commercializing female sexuality and reproduction, as well as a (to my thinking) more credible concern about the experimental nature of the medicine involved. It's certainly a more nuanced view, shorn of the polarizing language (phrases like 'female enslavement' and 'caste warfare' are gone, as are Frankenstein metaphors) and ever-lurking transphobia that made earlier feminist writing on reproductive technology seem not only extremist, but outright callous to the people involved. There is often an at-least-passing acknowledgement of the struggle involved in trying to build one's family, and usually a mention of how critical technology has been for gay- and lesbian-headed families. As such, it's a view that gets a decent amount of play, despite being just as ideologically driven as anything that came out of FINRRAGE. A documentary about surrogacy as baby-buying permanently screens on Amazon Prime, while a non-peer-reviewed study about the harms of donor-sperm conception on children, published by a researcher from a conservative think tank, was cited on radical feminist Reddit groups and covered approvingly on *Slate*, NPR, and other liberal, feminist-flavoured media. And the sentiments survive in a diluted, everyday form – like the friend of a friend, a not-especially-radical women's studies professor, who told me on Facebook that surrogacy 'undermines women's role in reproduction,' and the self-proclaimed feminist in an attachment parenting group I joined who proclaimed that it was gestation that made one a mother. In March 2018, a Liberal MP, Anthony Housefather, introduced a bill that would decriminalize paying for donor eggs, sperm, and surrogacy in Canada, bringing us into line with U.S. states where 3PR is legally commercialized. The decision was met with support from infertility advocates and the LGBTQ community – and scathing op-eds by two (fertile) feminist academics and one feminist journalist, who were concerned that lifting the payment ban would commodify women's body parts and lead to their exploitation.

There is something important in the trajectory from the apocalyptic warnings of FINRRAGE-era feminists to the more tempered anti-surrogacy feminists of today that I can't quite put my finger on. It worries at me, so one day, four months before the birth of my son, I decide to read through all of it. The early stuff I have to find in used bookstores or online. With their second-hand hardcovers featuring stock images of eggs and speculums and four-alarm, caps-lock-rendered titles (*Man Made Women*), they look as ominous as I expected; their brittle, transparent dust covers seem less like quaint reminders of their library-bookshelf pasts than attempts to protect me against the explosive content inside.

I read all the FINRRAGE reports I can find, and then all of the interviews with the FINRRAGE women, and, finally, all of the books. I read Janice Raymond, who likens IVF to 'medical pornography' and, echoing the clueless woman who suggests that her infertile friend just needs to 'be patient and try a little longer,' proposes that many infertile women are misdiagnosed and are perfectly fecund after all. I read Greer, who suggests that the infertility of Western women is psychosomatic in origin (infertile women in the Global South owe their troubles to diseases transmitted by sex with white men). I read Gena Corea, who argues that reproductive technologies 'represent an escalation of violence against women, a violence camouflaged behind medical terms.' And when Maria Mies seems to address me directly – 'Why don't you simply say … that this new technological development frightens you, that you don't need it, that it is inhuman and inimical to women and you won't buy it?' – I spend some time formulating a sincere answer (but I did need it, Maria!). I read dozens of accounts of surrogacy as womb-renting, as animal husbandry, as slavery (whatever issues I have with these writers, I can't deny them their flair with metaphor), all of which take for granted the non-capacity for the surrogate to freely consent. As Raymond writes, all consent under patriarchy is limited by the fact that the going choices for women a priori suck: 'consent does not simply amount to acquiescing to the available options.'

I do not expect to like any of this, and sure enough, I don't. But what surprises me is that it's not for the reasons I expect.

The technology created my family, but it also created my infertility in the first place (whether it was a D&C for my first miscarriage that caused it, or a fibroid removal surgery in 2014, I'm certain I wasn't born with scar tissue in my pelvis). The technology has left as many of my friends without children as with them. The technology turns every infertility support group into a de facto IVF cheering squad, with women urging each other through surgery after surgery, injection after injection, with the militaristic bromides to 'never give up' and 'remember the end goal' and 'it will all be worth it when you have a baby.' I was certainly as traumatized by the treatments I underwent as I was by my childlessness, so when radical feminists point out how this is partly baked into the technologies themselves, I find it difficult to object.

There is also the predictable insistence that infertile women are at best dupes of patriarchy and at worst its collaborators; this rankles, but not to the extent I expected. They are rightly critical, I think, of the tendency of the infertility industry to characterize IVF and other invasive technologies as 'family-building options' or, worse yet, to place such technologies in the realm of potentially liberating 'personal choices' (of all the ways I could characterize my relationship to IVF, it feels most disingenuous to describe something I did while experiencing five consecutive miscarriages as a *personal choice*). To be sure, I am pretty outraged by the false distinction these authors draw between marginalized and infertile women (as if there are no infertile poor women or women of colour! as if infertility were not also an axis along which women are marginalized!), and the wholesale selling out of single women, trans people, and gay men who can't biologically reproduce without some form of technological intervention (some of the writers allow lesbians to use an unpaid sperm donor and a turkey baster) –

but all of that is the stock and trade of conservative rhetoric about women; I'm used to it and it registers as white noise.

Ultimately, it's the ways in which radical feminism echoes the limiting ideas of motherhood and femininity in the first wave that feels so defeating to me. Despite their valorization of pregnancy and childbirth – the same essentialism that led many of them straight into professional transphobia – radical feminists share much with their early-twentieth-century foremothers. Linda Layne, writing about pregnancy loss, analyzes how, in the cornerstone radical feminist text *Our Bodies, Ourselves*, miscarriage and infertility are segregated into a chapter at the end of the book, far apart from the multiple chapters on pregnancy and childbirth. While the pregnancy and childbirth chapters assiduously normalize and humanize the experiences for the readers, featuring large photographs of laughing, labouring women and their newborns, the chapter on the 'rare and heartbreaking occurrence' of miscarriage and infertility is not illustrated at all. In addition to erasing women who experience these already-taboo events from the text (indeed, from the women's health movement as a whole), the decision, Layne writes, to segregate and de-face infertile and miscarrying women betrays an ideology rooted in the liberalism it claims to critique:

> Pregnancy loss contradicts two fundamental premises of the women's-health discourse of pregnancy and birth – that women can control their reproduction and that birth is a natural, joyful experience … An unintended and unexamined consequence of this is that women may be assumed to be responsible for their pregnancy losses. Despite the women's-health movement's sustained critique of biomedical models of reproduction, it in fact shares with biomedicine a belief in the ability to control

reproduction … so focused has the women's health movement been in challenging biomedine's pathologization of pregnancy and birth, it has systematically minimized and marginalized negative reproductive outcomes.

And yet this strand of second-wave feminism doesn't seem so gung-ho about women controlling their reproduction when the issue is an infertile woman who wants to reproduce. Despite its surface technophobia, the women's health movement shared with its first-wave progenitors an ardent advocacy for birth control and abortion (although the eco-feminists among them indeed promoted non-medicalized, 'natural' alternatives to these interventions). Like the eugenicists, they were selective about what kind of control was permissible, promoting technologies that allowed women to not have children, while either ignoring or opposing those that might help women have them. As ever, the desire to not be a mother is valid, while the desire to *be* a mother is rendered abject.

At least part of this is due to the extended critique of motherhood feminism had offered. Layne explains that in 'at least some feminist circles, members of pregnancy-loss support groups risk being condemned for their "maternal desire," and the anthropologists who study them may be castigated for "condoning" this desire.' She describes a review of a study she contributed to about foster, adoptive, and bereaved mothers as castigating these women for 'aspiring to be mothers within patriarchal culture.' Layne quotes American feminist theorist Carole Stabile, who put it this way: for some second-wave feminists, 'pregnancy [is] the ultimate act of female complicity, as the exemplar of feminine false consciousness.'

So why aren't women who easily conceive seen as complicit? As Layne explains, there is a double standard within feminism vis-à-vis maternal desire: 'the motivations of women who choose to bear children and do so without difficulty are not subject to the same feminist critique of those who try but fail.' In other words, only infertile women have maternal desire; they are not mothers but sites of effort, longing, and labour to reproduce. In contrast, the fertile woman is maternal, full stop. No desiring is needed; her maternity *just is*. The logic here is plain – the default state of woman is pregnancy and childbirth – and it is of course the oldest, rankest misogyny in the books. Reproduction and motherhood are supposed to happen *naturally* to women: naturally, instinctively, and easily (as evinced by the plethora of second-wave articles and books about the ease with which women should labour, birth, and breastfeed). When maternity is the subject of effort, labour, and desire, it is unnatural, and what does not happen naturally must be constructed. And what is constructed, especially under patriarchy, must be less valid.

Layne quotes British feminist scholars Birke, Himmelwiet, and Vines: 'Understanding where a need comes from does not remove it. Nor indeed is there any difference in the desire for children from any other in that respect. All needs and desires are socially produced.' But there is no attempt to trace the needs or desires of infertile women in the technophobic literature of the second wave; there are scant few instances in which our voices are included at all.

Contrast this to the current feminist work on infertility, much of which focuses on the abuses of surrogacy and egg donation. There is variety here: some critics are against the practices altogether, while others only seek to outlaw commercial (paid) egg and sperm donation as well as surrogacy. In most cases, however, there is an implied sympathy for the intended parents (those who will receive the donated sperm or egg or who contract the surrogate) and at least a tacit acceptance that our desire to have a family is valid. And yet, when I turn my attention to it – the hardcover 1980s books shelved, I screen documentaries and read articles and social media feeds online – I actually find it more troubling: more implicitly dismissive of infertile women, more sexist and essentialist.

Take, for example, the website Surrogacy 360, a watchdog organization for the international commercial surrogacy and egg donation industries run by the Boston Women's Health Collective, the same second-wave touchstone that produces *Our Bodies, Ourselves*. Purportedly addressed to people who might want to build their families this way, it avoids condemning intended parents who seek international surrogacy arrangements and instead focuses on ways they can help improve the social and legal experiences of donors or surrogates (for example, by insisting on the safer practice of transferring only a single embryo to the surrogate rather than the standard two or three). It's an excellent resource, and I've recommended it to people considering international surrogacy. But it's telling, I think, that it is produced by the BWHC, which has never addressed the particular struggles of women with infertility in any sustained way, let alone with the dedication they devote to egg donors and surrogates.

As I'm puzzling over this, I keep returning to their section on egg donation, a practice that is admittedly an ethical and legal mess: outcomes are not properly tracked; research is minimal; unscrupulous agencies misrepresent the process in ads designed to recruit donors. There is no doubt that egg donation is risky and falsely advertised, and that the business of it needs a complete overhaul. But what the site does not mention is that egg donors undergo the same medical process as infertile women retrieving their own eggs – superovulation and egg retrieval. Critics of egg donation who are nonetheless unconcerned with superovulation and egg retrieval itself often mention that donors with young, healthy ovaries are at an elevated risk for 'hyperstimulation' – a risky side effect of the drug regime – compared to older, infertile women. But the biggest risk factor for hyperstimulation is not, in fact, youth and health, but a very common infertility condition – polycystic ovary syndrome. And as for youth and health, around a third of women undergoing egg retrieval do so because their male partners are infertile and IVF is the only way to get a sperm into their egg. That feminists are concerned with the medical effects of egg retrieval on donors, but not on infertile women in the same demographic as donors, implies that they care more about fertile bodies than infertile ones. Considered in light of BWHC's overall silence about the experience of infertile women, the suggestion is difficult to ignore.

If contemporary critics of third-party reproduction appear more sympathetic to infertile women, it's in a surface way. A common criticism of surrogacy and/or egg donation is that it allows wealthy white infertile and queer couples to uphold the patriarchal, colonial idea of the biologically connected, two-parent, intraracial family – adoption is implied to be the more feminist choice. The difficulty of adoption aside – the years-long timelines, the open-ended outcome (some families do not get a child placed at all; others have 'failed adoptions,' in which the mother takes the child back; it can be just as expensive as surrogacy; it's notoriously difficult for single parents, gay couples, and trans people to adopt) – the adoption industry and foster-care system are arguably more colonial. In Canada, where I live, most adoptable children come from racialized backgrounds, and their mostly Indigenous birth families are often victimized by intergenerational trauma and oppression. (Including the trauma of ongoing state intervention in their intimate family lives, by the same institutional bodies that determine who qualifies as fit to parent in the first place). That some people might choose to create families via third-party reproduction rather than adoption or fostering, not because of genetics but because it might strike them as the *more* feminist (or the least unfeminist) choice, does not appear in this analysis.

These are all intellectual quibbles, though; mostly, when I read this work, I feel disoriented.

It's the tone of it – the bloodless, objective, anthropological approach to the question of me, and what to do about the feminist problem that is me – that makes it impossible for me to keep reading it in good faith. It is about me but not for me. I'm the object of these screeds; it's *literally* objectifying. It says something – though I'm not sure what – that I never felt the insult of being *objectified as a woman* more keenly than when I was infertile, reading feminist analyses of infertility.

Objectified in my absence: in framing us as problematic consumers of technology that they despise, both FINRRAGE-era and contemporary feminists make the same error as the patriarchal technocrats who, borrowing the liberty rhetoric of the liberal feminist abortion movement, promote IVF as a positive choice for 'building one's family.' They ignore the actual experience, the meat and pain, of infertility. They ignore the *grief*.

Four

H ere, from the *Cut, New York Magazine*'s fashion vertical, a
fairly standard way to open an article about infertility:

> Every woman who embarks on a cycle of in vitro fertilization
> is familiar with the ride: the multiple cycles of hormonal
> stimulation, the pain of the injections, the discomfort and
> the bloating; then the delicate harvest of eggs to be fertilized
> outside the body, and the anxious wait for genetic testing
> on the embryos to make sure they have the right number
> of chromosomes before they are transferred back; and then,
> if all of the embryo tests come back abnormal, or the
> embryos don't implant, or the pregnancy ends prematurely
> in miscarriage, the process starts all over again.

Rare is the third-person report of infertility that does not
begin in a clinic (if not literally inside the woman's body)
recounting, with a mix of amazement and faint disapproval,
the multiple ministrations and procedures involved in the
intervention. If the occasion for this intervention – female
infertility – is mentioned, it's in passing: as a medical diagnosis
(as here, the experience of miscarriage is dispensed with in
one clause) or, in the more explicitly critical stories, euphe-
mized as 'the thwarted desire to be a parent.' The grief and
isolation of infertility, and the gendered way these humiliations

are meted out, are secondary to what happens next: the numerous and painful tests and procedures, the extraordinary costs (tens of thousands in this story), and, above all, the technological sorcery of the researchers and physicians. Whether she is derided or pitied, in the era of IVF, the infertile woman first enters the public imagination not as a woman, not even as a patient, but as a consumer of biotechnology. A specific kind of consumer: the consumer as spectacle. With her grief reduced to a vague 'desire' for a baby, and the efforts of making this baby rendered as so extraordinary, so risky and costly and scientifically improbable, it's difficult to see her as anything other than a curiosity of capitalism, akin to people who undergo cosmetic surgery (who, it must be said, are also underserved by this rhetoric). Her grief is mundane and relatable, but we don't really hear about it. We hear about the technology, which is so astounding it may as well be from outer space (to wit, some headlines: 'IVF as Science Fiction'; 'The First Babies Conceived Through a Futuristic New Technology Have Already Been Born'; 'Adventures in a New World of Reproductive Technology'). I'd see stories like this, most often while paging through magazines in fertility-clinic waiting rooms, and the otherworldly, ephemeral language amused me. The science behind the treatments I've had might be far-fetched, but nothing could be more boring, more bodily and visceral and age-old, than their effect: my abdomen hurt, I was bloated and tired, and the skin on my stomach was criss-crossed with scars. Where an uninvolved reader might see high-tech genetic wizardry in fertility medicine, the patient knows foremost the discomfort of her body, the frustration of waiting, the possibility of a child – the dull terrain trafficked by all mothers. Unwritten in every account of IVF's technological spectacle is something boring but very key: here is a person who wants to have a baby but can't. As Doris Del-Zio, the first woman to undergo IVF in the United States, responded to her brief media celebrity: 'I didn't do it to be the first; I did it because I desperately wanted a baby.'

'You really wanted a baby,' people who have had no trouble conceiving sometimes say to me, thinking themselves supportive, affirming. And while I've tried many times to pinpoint why this offends me, there's an element I always have trouble explaining. It's not that it's trivializing; it's not that they have underestimated my grief. These people know very well that I was in deep grief, and I think they empathize with this and respect it. Rather, it's that they don't get the particular nature of this grief, how it's less about the loss of a potential child than it is about the endless possibility that there may yet be an actual child. For Freud, mourning is about a lost object; the grieving person has a type of hole in them, in the shape of the lost thing – their work in healing is to fill that hole with something else. I think that's still the standard understanding of grief: the person with their heart punched out, a woman with a baby-shaped hole in her head. But that pattern never with resonated me, or with the other infertile women I've discussed this with. If you drew me at the point of my most brutal need, I'd look less like a woman with a hole in me than I would like multiple identical women, a chain of paper dolls that had been cut but not yet pulled apart. Each of these dolls, these women, is living a separate life: some in which I went on as I was, childless, and others in which this or that procedure had worked and I had a baby. The women overlap; they are all *me*. But the edges where they diverge are paper-cut sharp. In all of my reading about grief, I never found an account that described this sensation better than the ones about dissociation – a near-psychotic awareness of myself as being multiple places, multiple women, at the same time. Infertility doesn't just isolate women from each other, it isolates us from ourselves.

Because, in a sense, there are many of each infertile woman – she is multiplied by her unique, acute sense of possibility and desire. The next procedure might work, the fallopian tube could always clear, the next fetus might not miscarry. In the words of our moms, *miracles happen*. It's not that motherhood is out of reach, it's that it's just out of reach. It's not that motherhood didn't happen, it's that it almost did and, in fact, still could. The difference between the grief of infertility and other reasons for mourning – the loss of a spouse, for example – is in that promise of 'just,' in 'almost,' in 'still could.' This does not make it more or less livable than other forms of grief, but it goes a long way toward explaining why it is expressed in ways that seem so desperate and even alien to the casual onlooker, why a woman might put herself under the knife ten, twelve, twenty times to get pregnant, why she might spend hundreds of thousands of dollars in the effort. The end to her grief is just so near. The tragedy of infertility is one of proximity, and the thing about this proximity is that it is partly created – and potentially solved – by technology.

The existential clusterfuck of this trauma is something that could never be captured by the common rhetoric around infertility – so present in the feminist literature on reproductive technology – that flattens the complex sufferings of infertile women into the (faintly misogynistic) image of a woman 'wanting to have a baby.' The rhetoric underestimates the extent to which, for many infertile women, continuing to try to have a baby, and wanting to try everything to have that baby, is less about 'having a baby' than it is about resolving that dissociation – getting back into that single body, that single self. It's less of a biological impulse than a narrative one, a need for coherence and sense. Australian feminist bioethicist Catherine Mills has proposed seeing reproductive rights as less about the event of having or not having children than about 'the freedom to make oneself according to various ethical and aesthetic principles or values'; reproduction is a project of self-making. And currently, the infertile woman, unmade by her grief, is presented with only one dominant narrative to remake herself: have a baby, either through miracle or science. That this narrative is culturally prescribed makes it no less visceral or real. I abandon the feminist critics of biotech, wondering less about what it means that they proscribed reproductive technology than what their accounts might have looked like had they admitted the particular nature of infertile women's grief.

In 1989, the same year as the FINRRAGE conference in Comilla, the Mulroney federal government convened a Royal Commission on New Reproductive Technologies, under the direction of geneticist and physician Patricia Baird. The commission was partly in response to years of lobbying on the part of the National Action Committee on the Status of Women – NAC for short – to address the massive growth of the IVF industry, surrogacy, commercial gamete donation, and genetic fetal technologies in Canada. An umbrella organization comprised of dozens of women's organizations, including domestic violence shelters, immigration activists, and First Nations women's groups, NAC was at the time considered the main face of Canadian feminism, roughly equivalent to the National Organization of Women in the U.S. However, while NOW had a largely liberal feminist bent – never, to my knowledge, issuing a policy statement about assisted reproduction – NAC was heavily influenced by socialist feminists who felt compelled to address, among the implications of the technology for women and the environment, the difficulty of 'informed consent' within a for-profit and largely unregulated medical sector. The Royal Commission, in the wake of the whiplash reversals of abortion legislation in the late 1980s, would spend $28 million and take four years before it published its final response to NAC's queries, a report called *Handle with Care* that ultimately took legislative shape in 2004. The policies based on *Handle with Care* form a largely incoherent system in which fertility treatment remains private and highly commercialized, surrogacy and gamete donation is legal but uncommercialized, and any public funds are directed to counselling or support for infertile women, let alone prevention or education – a stark contrast to the NAC recommendations. This is not surprising: while the Royal Commission was convened in response to NAC, no members of NAC were appointed to sit on it (Maureen McTeer, an honourary director of the Canadian Abortion Rights Action League, provided a liberal-leaning feminist voice, while the socialist-feminist professor Louise Vandelac was booted from the commission in its early years). Rather, the commission was made up of representatives from the infertility industry itself – doctors, bioethicists, as well as a few figures from the religious right (infertile women testified to the commission, but none were appointees).

What might the landscape of Canadian infertility have looked like if the most prominent feminist voices had shaped that report? I read the brief NAC provided to the commission, expecting a FINRRAGE-style blanket technophobia (not least because it is titled 'A Technological Handmaid's Tale'), the usual radical feminist dismissal of infertile women's perspective out of hand. I am not only surprised but a little rattled to find that I disagree with little of it; it is focused throughout on the validity of infertile women's grief. Its first sentence, in fact, asserts the 'agony of thousands of infertile women,' and it offers several cogent recommendations for solving female infertility in sustainable ways, through prevention and female health education. Most impressively, it recommends that the reproductive-technology industry be brought under the auspices of the government, both to improve regulations and data collection (partly as a result of the commission, data from fertility-clinic cycles is still only provided to the government by clinics on a volunteer basis) and to equalize access to these technologies for women of different socio-economic classes. While it calls for a moratorium on new IVF clinics, pending further research on medical outcomes, it does not suggest anything so simplistic as a ban. In other words, it was the socialist-feminist account of infertility I had never heard: a large-picture analysis that offered something much more interesting than an admonition against technology: a way to talk about infertile women as something other than consumers of IVF.

Over multiple hours of conversation, I speak with Varda Burstyn, the former chair of NAC's reproductive technology action group and the author of the brief. Now researching chemical pollutants independently from her home in Peterborough, Ontario, Burstyn had a long post-NAC career teaching women's studies, and there is much of the radical professor in her rapid-fire speech and frequent tangents into far-flung fields: ecology, film, religion. As she tells me, she is an infertile woman, the result of the Dalkon Shield, an IUD taken off the market in the 1970s after thousands of women filed injury lawsuits. But her focus is less on such risky technology itself than on the intricate social and economic history that has led more women than ever to face challenges while trying to conceive. She links the late-twentieth-century decline of the family wage – the collective expectation that one family member, usually the man, can and should earn enough income from a job to support the rest of the family – to declining social and legal protections for mothers and pregnant women in Western economies. The simultaneous rise of 'liberal masculinism' (a type of martini-swilling, commitment-averse, perpetually adolescent male in the mould of Hugh Hefner) and the birth-control pill (which severed sex from reproduction) created a culture that celebrated the sexually free young woman while degrading the figure of the mother as backwards and dull. A brand of consumer-oriented feminism, compatible with both liberal masculinism and neo-liberal economics, deprioritized issues facing mothers such as remunerating unpaid work in the home and access to affordable child care. The mainstream version of North American feminism thus took as its primary object a very specific type of woman: young, white, middle-class, able-bodied, and seeking access to birth control and abortion. The overall picture is one in which the mother – who she is, what she needs – disappears as a subject of both mainstream politics and popular feminist discourse: a large-scale de-maternalizing of modern culture.

Within this context, Burstyn asks, is it any wonder why female infertility would remain a taboo and misunderstood thing? Why women would feel forced to start families later and later, putting them at risk for miscarriage and infertility? (I think of an infertile woman quoted in the *New Yorker* as feeling 'sterilized' by student debt.) A society that does not protect mothers, that doesn't even see them, is hardly going to care about the woman who is trying to be a mother, the woman who is trying and failing. It makes sense that in what Burstyn terms an 'anti-maternal' capitalist culture, the figure of infertile woman would only come into public view after the fact, as a consumer of privatized reproductive technology.

'If you have a personal, individual encounter with the technology, it doesn't seem sinister,' Burstyn told *Toronto Life* in 1992.

> But if you step up from the level of the individual and look at the social aggregate, you get a very different impression. I don't judge any woman for wanting to have a child and possibly doing anything she can to have one, but I sure do judge medical scientists and pharmaceutical companies – which are the driving force behind these technologies – for putting into her path a technology that is dangerous to her health and *wildly ineffective*, which she will nevertheless want to try because of her desire to have children.

I get all of this – until I don't. There are still many pieces of me, feminist parts that are galvanized by analyses of infertility in the abstract and infertile parts that are ragged with grief. When I look at pictures of my son's ultrasound, or see the photos my friends post on social media – all IVF babies, surrogacy babies, babies born to gay dads and single moms who could only get those kids via reproductive technology – all the sane and interesting words vanish; there are only their smooth faces and the parents' smiles, relieved and amazed at their unlikely bounty.

Burstyn is right to point out the illusory nature of 'choice' under consumer capitalism – how women's capacity for consent is always pre-limited. It is a cornerstone insight of the reproductive-justice movement and a necessary move toward considering how women's choices always happen within the holistic context of our lives, tempered by race, class, sexuality, and gender. In this sense, I agree with her that 'the right to choose' is a flawed way to go about reproductive politics. Still, there is a risk of essentialism here. Feminist academic Nadia Mahjouri points out how the radical and socialist feminist critique of choice-based feminism can be oversimplifying. Discussing whether or not women's social circumstances cancel out our ability to freely choose reproductive technology, including paid surrogacy, she writes:

> If [...] as feminists, we want to hold that women can act autonomously in choosing whether or not to continue a pregnancy (despite the supposed potential emotional risks) so too must we accept that the surrogate can autonomously choose to enter a contractual agreement that requires taking both the supposed physical and emotional risks that contract pregnancy entails. Furthermore, to argue that women who agree to this process must in some way be coerced into it by the desperation of economic need is, as Diprose points out, to ignore the fact that this is the motivating factor for all labour projects undertaken in a capitalist society.

While the surrogate or infertile woman's 'choice' is thus limited by her circumstances, it is one of many similar choices. To single out these choices as particularly unfeminist or dangerous is to suggest that women are especially incapable of making decisions about their reproductive anatomy – a retread of the paternalistic logic that, first, defines the womb as the sacred and essential seat of womanhood, and then places it under public scrutiny and control.

Mahjouri is one of several new critics focusing on a more nuanced understanding of reproductive technology, and thus female infertility. Roughly working in the tradition of Donna Haraway and Judith Butler, she understands these technologies as neither bad nor good on their own, but, rather, new ways in which women can relate to their bodies that vary according to how they are used and to what ends. Focusing on the ways in which reproductive technology is employed allows us to go beyond discussions of 'bodies of women overcome, or dominated by technology' as well as women 'liberated from biology' but instead as 'bodies of agents – women who are negotiating their way through the difficult terrain that constitutes the reproductive process in a technological age.' This approach demands 'women remain central to this discussion – it places women's multiple and various needs, desires and experiences at the forefront, rather than leaving them, silenced, in the shadows of these debates.'

When we shift focus from the technologies themselves to illuminate the experiences of these women in the shadows, the problem that jumps out is less that we are being coerced to choose these things than the fact that we are not equally free amongst ourselves, reproductively speaking. Reproductive-justice activists are right to ask, are women of colour as free as white women, reproductively speaking? Their question clears space for mine: are infertile women as free as fertile women? In the anti-technology literature, even the more moderate work that only opposes itself to advanced technologies like sex selection or donor gametes, infertile women are held to a different, stricter standard than fertile ones. A standard criticism of egg and sperm donation is that it allows people to seek out donor eggs and sperm from people who are white, blue-eyed, well-educated, and so forth; little is ever said about fertile people who choose their mates (the prospective genetic parent of their children) for similarly superficial reasons (there is no more effective way of producing white elite babies than white elites, fucking). A woman undergoing IVF who has her embryos tested for sex so she can choose a boy or a girl is derided, while websites and books counselling people on how to naturally conceive this or that gender pass without comment. I believe most feminist critics of reproductive technology would admit that the racism and sexism of the infertility industry reflects the racism and sexism of our culture at large. But to task only infertile people with resolving those issues seems doubly unfair. In other words, why do fertile people get to conceive in all kinds of ethically dubious ways without interference, but not us?

The stock answer here is that one type of conception is natural and the other technological. But where do we draw the line between technology and nature? Is the pregnancy of a couple who are together because they met online, who are both alive because of a lifetime of vaccines and antibiotics, that was bookended by hormonal contraception and elective sterilization, and which will be monitored by ultrasound and amniocentesis, really more 'natural' than, say, that of an infertile couple who uses IVF to select a male embryo, or a lesbian couple who uses donor sperm? The line between 'natural' and 'technological' families is less self-evident than it is selective and evaluative, distinguishing acceptable ones (natural) from unacceptable ones (technological). I am as critical as any second-wave feminist about the ways in which the fertility industry has used technology to reinforce old, harmful ideas about gender, parenthood, and bodies. But is it feminist to allow women only 'natural' choices, when the category of 'natural' is so porous in the first place? Scrutinizing infertile people's motives for parenthood while fertile people remain beyond the scope of inquiry just reinscribes another, equally sexist idea: that infertile women's desires and needs should be treated with suspicion.

I wonder, here, if I am too close to the issue to see it clearly. If maybe I am selfish, and picking and choosing my politics to conform to my deep personal needs. Antifeminist journalists have a phrase for women who do this: *wanting it all*. It's a risable term – no one speaks of men 'wanting it all' – but something about it resonates now. Maybe I do 'want it all,' I think. By all, I don't mean a family-plus-job; I am ride-or-die with the idea that those two things are normal and reasonable expectations for an adult human. By 'all,' I mean a politics that I can get behind 100 per cent – a politics that serves exactly me. I want the parts of 1970s socialist feminism where female infertility is approached as a social as well as a medical issue, but not the parts where it means I can't have a family. I want the parts of Lean-In feminism where I can get IVF, but not the parts where I have to pretend that IVF was created or is practised with women's best interests in mind. My heart is only into the politics that serves it well, and there is no strand of feminism I find that will submit. What is politically good and what is good for me will always be two bodies that can't quite cohere, that overlap mostly but not all the way. While I'm not surprised that I too was cheated by the incompleteness of the old feminist slogan *the personal is political*, what is surprising is how much it feels like grief.

I met my friend Kylie in a Reddit group devoted to radical feminists who spend the vast majority of their time mocking transgender women, whom they consider non-women due to their absence of uteruses and ovaries, xx chromosomes, socialization in the male gender role, or some combination thereof. Occasionally, almost as a fun diversion, they turn their attention to the threats of sex work and pornography, or reproductive technology (surrogacy, mostly). While Kylie completed her transition almost ten years ago and passes perfectly, almost every aspect of her life has been impoverished by transphobia: she has been fired from jobs, assaulted, and alienated from former friends and family. Trans-exclusive radical feminists, or TERFS, may play a small role in modern feminist politics, but they have loomed large for her, opposing legislation that would ensure her civil rights, writing mocking op-eds in major newspapers, and, in one case, brigading her Facebook page with memes and GIFs calling trans women rapists and oppressors. Despite all of this, she is a committed feminist. She attends protests, has volunteered at women's shelters, and still spends a lot of time debating misogyny on her social media and on forums like the one where we met.

I do not want to understate our difference – I am an upper-middle-class, straight, cisgender woman; she is a young, queer, trans woman who struggles for a livable income. But there is something telling in the fact that Kylie and I first connected as feminists even though mainstream feminism, devoted as it is to the concerns of a normative type of woman, has largely ignored the major struggles we've both faced as women. And within this, many self-identified feminists continue to oppose and vilify strategies that help trans women and infertile women. Feeling excluded from a discourse that we were both passionate about remains a powerful point of alignment for us, and – ironically, perhaps – a point of solidarity as women.

Although there is this vocal contingent of feminists who maintain that she does not belong in a women's change room, let alone a women's movement, Kylie is what I think of when I imagine a modern feminist – as well as the person I go to when I want to try to hash out my own thoughts about feminism vis-à-vis my own life. I put a question to her on one of our regular late-night chats:

'Do I think infertility is important because I'm a feminist, or did I just really want to have a baby?'

She responds jokingly, with a meme: 'Why not both?' Then, more seriously: 'I don't think you can separate them. You wanted to have a baby, and that shaped your politics. Isn't that how everyone works?'

But what about the parts where my politics and my personal longings diverge?

Maybe, she says, that's where it ends. Maybe part of being a feminist is just finding a way to be comfortable with the gap between politics and desire, accepting that there is a way in which feminism will never solve our personal agonies and was never meant to. But doesn't that let too many people, myself included, off the hook? I think about the ways in which, within feminism, some women's 'personal' longings and griefs have always been considered more worthy of attending to – of politicizing – than others'. And who, as a result, become worthy of the particular healing, both social and individual, that feminist politics, at its best, has always offered.

Politicizing women's intimate grief isn't just feminist because it can get stuff done policywise, it's feminist because it can restore to a woman a full story and a new role as the teller of that story. Grief is inevitably an experience of fragmentation, unwholeness, incoherence. In grief, a woman is divvied up; she is not herself. But when I think of the feminist women I have admired, such as those I saw online at the women's march, what amazes me is – despite whichever form of grief accompanied them there – how present they are, how solid. They were rooted not only to each other, it seemed, but also within themselves. Each marcher took up not only physical space, but also narrative space: she was someone whose story, whatever it was – sexual assault, abortion, harassment – was not only coherent, but so recognizable to others it could be invoked in the space of a placard.

Making women's stories visible is no small feat. Historian David Morris has pointed out that 'male pain tends to play itself out in open public spaces (football stadiums, combat fields, streets), whereas female pain is relegated to private, closed spaces and the self-containment of a female body.' By grieving publicly, and witnessing one another's grief, women like those at the march make their stories of pain as visible and worthy of attention and redress as men's. The hashtag #believe-women is deceptively simple, going beyond the usual tokeniz-ing of women's experiences to get at a more holistic feminist ethics. It is the difference American feminist ethicist Kelly Oliver (incidentally an opponent of advanced reproductive technology) defines between recognition and witnessing. If recognition is the token political act of acknowledging the marginalized, 'witnessing' their struggle is ongoing, dynamic, and responsive. The whiff of metaphysics here is important: 'witnessing' means both the judicial act of 'seeing first-hand' and the religious one of bearing testimony to what is unseen – a miracle, say. The imperative of #believewomen picks up on this latter meaning, asking feminists and allies not just to *listen* to women, but to *believe* them – to witness 'in faith' trauma we can't see or materially verify. Feminism as spiritual praxis.

'I agree,' Kylie writes. But I know without seeing it that, as she writes this, she is shrugging. The problem, as she sees it, is how do you get people to make that leap of faith in the first place? Some women are automatically believed more than others (the root of transmisogyny, after all, is that trans women are not believed as women). So what to do about *that*?

'I don't know,' I say. I don't.

We both shrug into our laptops, a province apart.

After I log off, I reread a passage from Judith Butler's essay 'Violence, Mourning, Politics,' a widely cited account of the feminist potential of grief. She talks about public grief, how the act of witnessing grief sutures the onlooker to the mourner:

> When we lose certain people, or when we are dispossessed from a place, or a community, we may simply feel that we are undergoing something temporary, that mourning will be over and some restoration of prior order will be achieved. But maybe when we undergo what we do, something about who we are is revealed, something that delineates the ties we have to others, that shows us that these ties constitute what we are, ties or bonds that compose us. It is not as if an 'I' exists independently over here and then simply loses a 'you' over there, especially if the attachment to 'you' is part of what composes who 'I' am. If I lose you, under these conditions, then I not only mourn the loss, but I become inscrutable to myself. Who 'am' I, without you? When we lose some of these ties by which we are constituted, we do not know who we are or what to do. On one level, I think I have lost 'you' only to discover that 'I' have gone missing as well.

The mourner is 'undone' by her loss; her identity is fractured and remade in the absence of whatever is now gone. When we witness this, Butler says, we are not only forced to witness our own vulnerability, our own interdependence with others – a recognition that underlies all acts of empathy – but, in fact, we become part of that grief. The witness becomes one of the objects by which the mourner remakes herself, heals, and thus becomes responsible for her, in an act that is inherently political. And the witness, too, is transformed.

If any two women are sutured together in that Butlerian, political way, it's Kylie and I. When we met, we were both grieving – her, the diminishment of romantic possibility, safety, and respect in a world that was hostile to her, and me, my fertility and several miscarriages. These different but co-occurring struggles came to form the dark material of bonding and, later, the stuff of shared politics. We defended each other on message boards and social media. We both learned rarified medical terminology: I, of medical transition, and she, of surrogacy and IVF. She was the first female friend I told when I had an ectopic pregnancy, and later, a positive pregnancy test with our surrogate; a couple months later, when she fell unexpectedly in love – requited love! – with a wonderfully compatible person in her friend group, I championed that news in return. Our investment in each other necessarily meant that we were doggedly attentive to the politics, including the TERFy feminist politics, that invalidated each of us. I spent the last year paying as much attention to the passage of C-16, a federal bill that created protections for transgender people in Canada, as I did to provincial legislation that made it easier for me, rather than the woman who was my son's gestational carrier, to be registered as his mother at birth.

In other words, my friendship with Kylie was a political friendship, a specifically feminist political friendship – in the 1970s, we might have called each other sisters. But referring to it that way now feels a little too grand. Whenever I argued for her right to use a women's restroom or be acknowledged as a feminist, I wasn't doing that because of my abstract, feminist beliefs in trans rights, I did it because she was my friend. That her experience might be shared by trans women as a group was something I thought of after the fact; mostly, I was sad for her. If my politics aligned with the agreed-upon mainstream politics for trans-inclusive feminists, it was as a secondary effect.

But maybe that's a decent way to go about feminism. To believe in someone else's grief because you've seen them grieve.

To believe another woman when she says, 'This is what would help me.' Maybe, as Butler suggested, public acts of grieving can generate empathy and solidarity on their own, as unwelcome as they may be at first.

My relationship with Kylie was a small, private example of a feminist politics of grief – a politics centred on the whole woman, with all her intersections of oppressions and privileges and traumas and strengths. We had watched each other grieve over many months, seeing not only the more intense moments of confusion and pain but the ones in which we felt pretty good, and then all the in-between moments, too. We sat with one another (granted, mostly virtually) as we discussed our low points, but also things that were completely unrelated – we traded articles, we workshopped her paintings, we talked about books and movies and joked about dating. We saw one another in the interstices of grief. Grief tells a person's story – not only about what they have lost, and how, but about why losing that thing was so painful for them, what values and dreams and other stories were also compromised by that loss.

But this story can't be apprehended in one moment of feeling, it's a much longer and harder project. In my grief, I was many women; I was divvied up. But Kylie could see a more coherent tale, through witnessing it. The narrative of my grief rested with her, in her. She had my story even when I didn't. I felt like a fragment, but within her I was whole.

Five

Catherine Opie is, to me, the person who most embodies the idea that witnessing grief is a feminist act. Opie is an establishment photographer with write-ups in the *New Yorker* and a retrospective at the Guggenheim, but her roots are in the underground of radical queerdom: her most famous work captures the subversive, often ambivalent pleasures of being an out lesbian in the art and BDSM scenes of the eighties and nineties. Ambivalent in large part because what threads together each humanizing portrait – butch and femme and trans; naked and clothed and tanned and tattooed; embracing one another or posing solo – is an unmistakable theme of grief. In contrast to the sanitized images of lesbians in the early era of queer rights – the leather community was exiled from a gay-rights march Opie attended early in her career; a prime-time-ready Ellen DeGeneris was the acceptable face of lesbianism – her images palpate with not only defiance but its costs: a longed-for domesticity, the impossibility of family, the risks involved in choosing to have the children one wants in a culture that mandates otherwise. In 1993's *Self-Portrait/ Cutting*, Opie stands with her naked back to the camera, displaying a freshly rendered image on her skin: two stick figures, holding hands, in front of a house, and behind that, a spoke-wheel sun peeking out from behind a scallop-edged cloud. It is a child's drawing of a happy couple, a scene of clichéd American domestic triumph, but for two differences: the couple is two women, and the scene is cut into her back and dripping new blood. It registers Opie's primal, visceral longing for that second skirted stick figure – and the simple joys of romance, sunny yard, house – but also the figure that is only implied, the child in whose primitive hand the scene is carved. Whether the cutter is supposed to be Opie as a girl, naively drawing the family of her dreams, or the couple's implied child drawing her happy moms, the missing child – the *impossible* child – is the driver of the scene, the medium through which Opie's pain and longing is inscribed.

In two linked, subsequent pieces, the maternal and domestic grief of *Self-Portrait/Cutting* evolves. *Self-Portrait/ Pervert*, from 1994, features Opie in a leather fetish mask with piercings studding her folded arms and 'Pervert' carved along her breastbone. In contrast to the earlier piece, this image is more angry and self-effacing than it is wistful and sad. The child artist is gone, replaced by a calligrapher who works in an ornate, colonial-era script. The suggestion is that the adult Opie is not resisting, but absorbing the pathology that mainstream culture imposes on women like her in order to exclude them from the legal institutions of marriage and parenthood. But the conclusion of the trilogy, *Self-Portrait/Nursing*, photographed ten years later, could not be more poignant: Opie, face visible now, breastfeeding her toddler son – conceived via artificial insemination with her partner, Julie Burleigh, when she was forty – in the iconographic pose of Madonna and Child. The 'Pervert' scarring is still observable on her chest, yet it is faded; while her face is finally visible to the camera, it is directed at her son, not the viewer. It is gloriously optimistic without being sentimental. The foreground of the photo is occupied by the child in his mother's arms, but the grief of those family-less years is still present in Opie's lingering scars; in a literal way, the scar tissue is the background and foundation of the maternal scene itself.

I do not mean to suggest that Opie's *Self-Portrait* series is about infertility; that would diminish its power, which comes from the particularities of her grief, the specificity of being a kinky butch lesbian longing for domesticity and maternity in the age of the AIDS epidemic and 'Don't ask, don't tell.' The punishments and humiliations for queer and lesbian women have always been infinitely swifter and harsher than those for women like me. Doubly so for queer women who are also infertile: many states, for example, still discriminate against same-sex couples who seek to adopt; international adoption and surrogacy is notoriously difficult for everyone but married heterosexual couples; and the fertility world is still stubbornly heteronormative.[3] But the way in which she foregrounds her longing for children, her fears that this is impossible, and her eventual sublimation of grief into the bodily work of mothering, resonates more broadly. It makes a point about maternal longing and grief that I rarely see: how bodily it is, how it hurts, how hurting and grieving in this way is really hard work.

This idea – that motherhood is not a mode of being but varied practices of work – comes from Sara Ruddick, whose 1989 *Maternal Thinking: Toward a Politics of Peace* argues that mothering is an important mode of political and ethical thought. '[Mothers] are not identified by fixed biological or legal relationships to children,' she writes, 'but by the work they set out to do … The concept of mothering as a kind of caring labor undermines the myth that mothers are "naturally" loving.' Ruddick deconstructs the Victorian lodestar of maternal instinct, in which a mother's labour is figured as instinctive, automatic, and as unthinking as an animal's, as well as the second-wave feminist construction of the 'natural' and effort-less Mother Goddess. Instead, she argues that mothering is a set of practices as intellectual, thoughtful, complex, and elevated as the professional and creative work historically reserved for men. Separated from the idea of a 'natural' identity rooted in the female body, mothering work does not even need to be done by women, or even by one person; provocatively, she distinguishes pregnancy and child-bearing ('birthwork') as distinct from mothering. 'How can we celebrate the creative act of birth,' she asks, 'without reromanticizing an instinctive bonding, thereby denying the ambivalent responses of many birthgivers to their infants and the richly various arrangements in which lesbian, gay, and hetereosexual women and men take up maternal work?'

When I read Ruddick, I am electrified. Could the grief and longing that precedes conception – for many women, including women for whom conception seemed impossible, women like Opie and Kylie and me – also be a type of work? I think about how so many conventions and taboos around mothering obscure the fact that it is laborious, intentional, deliberate, and hard. Ruddick traces this sanitization of motherhood to Christian conceptions of childbirth:

In the Christian language … – 'glad tidings,' 'a child is born' – the physical realities of birth are at best passed over. The infant, quickly 'wrapped in swaddling clothes,' is quite unlike the crying, shitting, burping, sometimes colicky babies that I have known. His mother is even less bodily. Sexually innocent, clothed in spotless robes, she sits serenely with her child after a birth apparently attended only by her husband, a birth whose dangers and pains require no mention. Such a conception of birth denies the bodily realities on which the birth relationship depends, and this renders natality sentimental.

The most subversive thing a birthing mother can still do is reveal these bodily realities: breastfeed in public; post a naked selfie while pregnant; display a sagging and stretchmarked body that does not look sufficiently 'post-baby.' In the birthing mother's body is the history of pain, effort, sexuality, and, crucially, work. Mothers are also expected to conceal the labour they perform outside of pregnancy and birth; witness the social media trend of 'mom-shaming' women — often poor women and women of colour – who have accidentally revealed a messy or chaotic home, toted a crying child into a supermarket, or otherwise failed to create a Pinteresty mirage of effortless maternity. This is bog-standard misogyny that reveals, as Ruddick writes, that 'something troubling is being kept at bay' – the fact that motherhood is not an automatic role a woman passively accepts but an ongoing act of agency, effort, and commitment. We are disgusted by mothers who show this effort, and I wonder if it is for the same reasons that we also don't much like women who are struggling to have babies. The cliché thirtysomething single woman who is 'baby crazy,' or taking steps to have one that don't involve heterosexual sex with her husband, is pretty much the opposite of the 'natural mother,' for whom maternity is inevitable and automatic.

To a larger extent, the prohibition around displaying the work of motherhood reflects our larger distaste for exposing the labour behind femininity in general. Few people would dispute when pressed that much of femininity and masculinity comes down to learned practices; in modern feminist parlance, it is *constructed*. But a less-discussed point is how masculinity is more accepted as such than femininity. The project of masculinity is ongoing and public: we tell men to 'be a man' or 'man up'; men sculpt their bodies openly and publicly, speak of 'bro-ing out,' join groups and courses marketed to teach them 'masculine' skills, from hunting to seducing women.

No such phrases exist for women, who are maligned whenever they expose the seams of feminine artifice by revealing a strict diet, hair extensions, or cosmetic surgery, a seductive persona that is calculated or obviously learned. Transgender feminist Julia Serano has pointed out that much of transmisogyny comes down to how trans women reveal this contradiction: in their obvious self-construction as feminine, they remind us, uncomfortably, of how all femininity is a process of learning and labour. Our collective discomfort over infertile women's efforts to conceive, and mothers who display the blood and mess and difficulty of birthing and caring for children, is a similar affront to what Simone de Beauvoir identified as the organizing dichotomy of gender: masculinity is transcendent, projected outward to the realm of effort, action, and progress, and femininity is imminent: passive, inward, natural. 'Man' is a thing you work toward and become, while 'woman' just is.

Ruddick's insights became a foundational text in a new field of feminist scholarship, Motherhood Studies, established in 1997 by York University's Andrea O'Reilly. I spoke with one of her students, Sarah Sahagian, a cultural critic and PhD student, about how infertility might figure in.

'There's some writing on infertility in Motherhood Studies, but not much,' she says, adding that there's a lot to think about in terms of how the silence around infertility might link to the larger invisibility of motherwork. While this may seem counterintuitive – it's patriarchy, after all, that designated motherhood as the most natural and correct mode of womanhood – it reveals how invested we are in maternity as something that should *just happen* to women, rather than something they choose or work for. 'Infertility is portrayed as the punishment for women living a feminist-friendly life,' she explains. It's no coincidence that so much stereotyping around the 'bad mother' in patriarchal discourse is also coded as feminist or at the least unfeminine: the bad mother is self-involved, often works outside the home, is insufficiently self-sacrificing and deferent. She is a woman replete with the qualities we accept only in men: action, confidence, assertion, effort.

Thanks to interventions like Motherhood Studies and vocal activists who are feminists as well as mothers, mothers' rights are no longer the orphan issues of the feminist movement. Online and IRL, women applaud one another for public breast-feeding and posting their nude maternity photos. Articles advocating for subsidized child care, paid maternity leave, and publicly funded pre- and post-natal care appear regularly in mainstream feminist publications and under the bylines of feminist writers working for prestige media. Images that display the work of maternity, the stretchmarks and milk stains, the disorderly homes and sticky hands, go viral on social media under a variety of encouraging hashtags: #Ipumpedhere, #normalizebreastfeeding, #realparenting. Yet the work of infertility, the labour of grief and longing, is still largely invisible within feminism, which, at best, hews to the mainstream narrative of infertile women as the privileged consumers of reproductive medicine and, at worst, construes our maternal desire as a sign of patriarchal collusion. After years of searching for feminist discussions that seemed even passingly familiar with women's actual experiences of infertility, the best one I've found, and the one I still come back to, is buried in the infertility subgroup of Reddit, among anonymous posters whose identities I can't even guess at.

But it is, truly, a fantastic thread, with the electrical-storm quality of the best classroom discussions I've been in, an ever-accelerating exchange of anger-charged insights and off-the-cuff confession, and sincere, if unlikely, calls to action. The original post, quoted here in full, captures the infertile feminist's sense of loneliness and betrayal:

> I feel like I've been in my hour of need for years now and feminism is nowhere to be found. If I wanted/needed to have an abortion, not have an abortion, breast-feed, not breast-feed, stay home with a kid, not stay home with a kid, get paid maternity leave, get paid paternity leave, feminism would have my back with 1000 articles and slogans and websites and supportive narratives for why that is a great choice. But infertility? Facing a devastating, gendered medical diagnosis, with no insurance coverage, while battling bullshit misogynistic social narratives at every turn? Fuck you kid, you're on your own.
>
> I did a literature search once for feminist theory and infertility, and you know what I found? An academic feminist's paper about how IVF is a tool of the patriarchy because it colludes politically weak women into 'breeding.' FUCKING THANKS. Last year, the leftist magazine the *Baffler* had an article, written by a woman, about how sad and weird it is for couples to pursue donor eggs, and it ended with a sanctimonious 'just adopt' anecdote about some lady who adopted like 8 special-needs kids from foster care. AGAIN, THANK YOU SO MUCH FOR THE SUPPORT AND SOLIDARITY. It's not just that feminism doesn't have my back, it's that I don't have to look hard to find feminists actually shitting on me.

It was one of the most active discussions on the subreddit that year, with dozens of pissed-off infertile women pointing out hypocrisies like student health plans that cover Viagra and penis pumps for erectile dysfunction, but not basic ovulation monitoring, or how feminists have focused on regressive personhood laws as a threat to abortion rights, while the same laws would also threaten a woman's right to IVF (embryos created by IVF are often not used or destroyed; if embryos had the legal status of persons, these routine practices would, as with abortion, constitute murder). Or how even the establishment feminist slogans 'pro-choice' and 'right to choose' imply the non-existence of infertile women, whose reproductive status is not a choice at all. Many agreed that there was a fundamental misogyny at work, an assumption that 'women's bodies are a wilderness, or nature that somehow "should be" out of the reach of medical care,' and that pregnancy and motherhood are the default states of womanhood:

> Motherhood itself is elevated (but not supported), but its essence is still considered one of sacrifice, that allows those who enjoy it moral superiority without ever addressing the question of whether or not they wanted children, and are exercising self-determination in having them.
>
> Since wanting your own children (whatever that means to you) and seeking infertility treatment isn't self-sacrificing, it denies society's definition of the essence of motherhood even while embracing it.

In other words, feminism has failed to recognize how infertile women embody so many of the abstract principles it fights for. In our efforts to conceive, we demonstrate the deliberate, conscious parenthood that is the purported goal of the reproductive rights movement. Our barrenness is a living rebuke to the idea that pregnancy is the 'natural' and inevitable state of all women. Erasing infertile women from feminism doesn't just alienate us, it impoverishes the movement. Another poster responds:

> We should be allowed to relish that desire for life. I don't want to approach this as a meager plea for crumbs, full of self-immolation, with the idea that I must remain in a constant state of atonement and self-sacrifice. For what? To fit someone else's stupid motherhood ideal? I want my super powers!
>
> Women pay mightily for their reproductive powers, and I want to enjoy them. I want to say, 'I did that. I wanted it, I sought it, I fought for it, I did what was needed to make it happen, and I won!' I want women in general to talk about wanting children as if it is something worth achieving instead of some mysterious hormonal illness that women are subjected to. I want to, someday, look clear-eyed at my child and say, 'You are here because I fought for you. Please always know how powerfully you are wanted, how important it was/is to me to get the chance to be your mom.'
>
> Cancer victims are allowed to 'fight.' The truth is that we are all fighters here. And fighting for *our* reproductive choice is feminist as fuck.

So what do we do? We make it visible, several say. We erode the stereotype of the infertile woman as patriarchal colluder, or the IVF consumer as privileged and daft, by countering with our real experiences.

> Maybe it's our responsibility to tell feminism to shut up and listen, because these are women's issues. We're not all Mombie wannabes. Some of us are strong, powerful,

passionate women who want to bring up strong and powerful children. The entirety of motherhood isn't a fucking Pinterest page.

We show them the work involved in our grief and our attempts to conceive, and the ways in which our concerns are part of the fabric of reproductive rights:

I've decided to be super-out with my IF journey. All the nitty gritty details to anyone who wants to hear them. Every hooch wanding. Every injection. Every 2 hour drive to my 8AM monitoring appointment, followed by another 2 hour drive home. Everything.

So people understand that when they're talking about the 'personhood' bill, or that BS in my home state (TN) that would make a child born with donor sperm an 'illegitimate' child that would have to be adopted by my husband. Even early abortion rights.

Because once my very much wanted pregnancy ended with no fetal heartbeat, I couldn't bear the psychological trauma of walking around with it still inside me for weeks and weeks until it naturally miscarried. I needed access to misoprostol – the so-called 'morning after' pill.

Decisions people make about other women's bodies have such far reaching and often little understood ramifications for others. The more my super conservative friends and family hear about my struggle, the more they are exposed to the idea that a soundbite about dead babies is only a tiny piece of the picture.

For Catherine Opie, grief and maternal longing took the form of a child's painting of family, an idealized domestic image weaponized by its inaccessibility. For Frida Kahlo, whose infertility was the result of a childhood accident that scarred her pelvis, grief is expressed at the scene of the crime, a hospitalization in a Boston institution after she miscarried a wanted baby. As Opie's queerness and kinkiness saturate her grief in the *Self-Portrait* series, Kahlo's experiences as a woman in post-colonial Mexico colour *Henry Ford Hospital*. The 1932 painting borrows the iconography of *retablos* or *ex-votos*: small devotional paintings on tin that narrate scenes in which a sick person, often depicted convalescing or being treated at a hospital, is healed through the off-scenes work of the Virgin or Christ. But in Kahlo's rendering, her first painting on tin, the sufferer in her blood-soaked medical bed floats apart from the hospital, which is part of an industrial skyline behind her. Clutching her abdomen, the Mexican woman is being pulled to the foreground of the composition by six large objects attached to her abdomen by umbilical-like red cords: an outsized, fully formed fetus, an anatomical model of a female pelvis, a skeleton of a female pelvis, an autoclave (a device for sterilizing medical instruments), an orchid (given to her by her husband after she miscarried), and a snail (an Aztec symbol of fertility that Kahlo said also symbolized how slow the process of miscarrying was).

While the woman is in the material space of the Western hospital, which sanitizes and depersonalizes her experience (the brand of 'Henry Ford Hospital' is stamped around the bottom rim of the bed), she is also in the bloody and bodily symbolic space of grief. This space has little to do with the regular world, tethered as mourners are to the objects of their suffering, images suffused with private and personal meanings. For Kahlo, as for all of us, the grief of miscarriage has its own language: a type of chant or repetitive drone: *what about my husband; why is it so slow; I can still see my baby*. It's as relevant to the experience of miscarriage now as it was in Kahlo's time, foregrounding the strangeness of women miscarrying in hospitals, which specialize in healing body parts (the model pelvis), not attending to the holistic experience of grief. Unlike in traditional *ex-votos*, the image of the Virgin is missing; her loss is happening in a spiritual void, removed from her culture and its penetrating symbols. The implication is that Kahlo is having a spiritual experience without spiritual support.

In her subsequent 1932 lithograph *Frida and the Miscarriage*, however, Kahlo registers more hope that her infertility might be given meaning through the sublimating process of art. There is no institutional hospital here, no sterilizing device or model of a pelvis – just a naked woman, crying and standing, with two fetuses: one tethered to her leg and another within her abdomen. To her right is a diagram of the cell division that drives early human growth – the inexorable processes of successful life that have abandoned her – and to her left, an ecosystem of plants whose roots are being fed from the blood dripping from her smaller left leg (in addition to the accident that injured her pelvis, Kahlo had polio in childhood that retarded growth in that leg). A stamen-like artist's easel grows out of the left side of her torso, and above her head, a human-featured moon, perhaps Ixchel, the Mayan goddess of the moon and childbirth. Kahlo biographer Hayden Herrera sees *Frida and the Miscarriage* as a sign of acceptance, writing that 'the painting is an antidote to maternal failure, that for Frida, making art must replace making children.'

But Kahlo's maternal desire is still there, as much present as it was in *Henry Ford Hospital*. She is still weighted down by the lost child she is tethered to; there is still a baby inside her. What's different is that the sterile institutional setting is gone, replaced by a network of life directly connected to

Kahlo's body and pain. Kahlo and her grief are embedded in the actual world. While in the earlier painting, the conventional image of a caring Virgin Mary is missing, here, female divinity is foregrounded: the moon stares at Kahlo and cries for her. This is not a painting about the importance of moving on but about how miscarriage, overmedicalized and socially taboo, separates women from the world and isolates them from the tools of healing: spiritual support (moon); practical knowledge (cell-division diagram); free licence to express their grief (artist's palette).

There is labour in Opie's and Kahlo's works. The bodily labour of Opie's incisions and piercings, Kahlo's bloody miscarriages and recovery; the emotional labour of both their longing and healing; the artistic labour that went into the creation of the pieces themselves. But more surprising is the labour their images demand of the viewer. Opie's portraits recall the formal portraiture of sixteenth-century painter Hans Holbein. 'I'm just going to sit here like Henry VIII in Hans Holbein's paintings and that's what you're going to have to deal with,' Opie told CNN. 'Think about Holbein and you are going to have to think about this image.' Opie compels her viewer to not only imagine her personal grief, but to reimagine art history itself through this grief, forever noticing the queer bodies and queer grief absent from its landscapes. It's not just queer sexuality and pain Opie seeks to transform, but a history that has erased these things. In contrast, Kahlo's miscarriage images task the viewer with a narrative job, asking us to assemble a story by putting together the fragmentary images and symbols she scatters through her foregrounds, making the pieces into a kind of sense. The viewer is forced, in a way, to retell the story of Kahlo's miscarriage – not *any* miscarriage, but specifically the miscarriage of this disabled Mexican female painter, this specific woman in this specific time and place. She is compelled to consider not just miscarriage, but what a miscarriage might mean in the context of any one woman's particular life.

I looked at Opie's portrait series and Kahlo's miscarriage works frequently when I was struggling, not so much because they mirrored my own experience or made me feel less lonely, but because I was heartened by what I felt was a complexity of their stories, a complexity missing in both my online support groups and the popular-media representations of infertility. They demonstrate the myriad nature of maternal grief, which the ancients seemed to get right: Lamashtu with her seven names and shape-shifting form. For Opie's grief is also the grief of being erased from history and from her own subculture; Kahlo's longing is part and parcel of her yearning for a pre-colonial cultural symbolic. Considering their work as an infertile woman, I'm reminded of my specificity, too, of how infertility might resonate differently in the life of a Latinx woman, a disabled woman, a queer woman, a kinky woman. I feel best compelled to witness such grief – to consider it, to hold it, to believe it – when I can observe it in the context of a woman's whole life, alongside all the other things she's been and done.

Conclusion

Jeremy and I met the woman who would give birth to our son in January: bleak weather, waning hope. For almost five years, we had been on what insiders call a 'surrogacy journey,' which was torturously long and complicated. In Canada, unlike the U.S. and India, surrogacy is largely unregulated, with prohibitions around payment. Even discussing paying a surrogate can net the parents up to ten years in prison and/or a $500,000 fine. But without the ability to legally compensate surrogates for pregnancy, few women in Canada offer to do it. The result is that many intended parents wait years to match, even with the services of paid 'consultants' who work to match waiting would-be parents with women willing to carry pregnancies for the cost of monthly expenses.

After having 'journeyed' with a paid consultancy for almost a year – during which time we received no matches – we had been connecting with prospective surrogates ourselves, using websites and our own personal connections. Our first, and then our second, surrogates each miscarried our three remaining embryos in turn, before deciding not to continue. Around the same time, I had an ectopic pregnancy that required surgery. My infertility felt less like the absence of something than a malignancy, spreading from one part of my body to the next, from me to these other women who tried to help.

We went back to the Canadian consultancies, who gave us a timeline of a year-long wait to match with a surrogate. With the additional time of legal and medical screening, it could be two years before we brought home a child. I wasn't sure I had the stamina for that. The remaining options were also grim: an American surrogacy would take less time but cost up to $200,000; the surrogacies overseas, in places like India or Kenya, were legally murky, and while the conditions of the surrogates likely varied, we were uncomfortable with not being able to confirm first-hand that the women were consenting, healthy, and had adequate control over their pregnancies. The risk of a failed adoption – where the birth mother takes the child back during the early stages of a placement, an occurrence far from uncommon in our province – still rendered adoption a non-starter. Out of embryos and nearly out of cash, with my womb in literal tatters and no other womb in sight, Jeremy and I spent our Christmas holiday trying to imagine which was more difficult: a year-long wait to even try for a baby, or a future as a family of two.

In my initial panic, I had emailed a number of family members and friends, asking if they knew anyone who could help. It was a desperate email, and one I'd sent many times to no avail, so I didn't think about it much after I pressed 'send.' But then, as I was fear-googling American surrogacy expenses, an email popped up from an address I didn't recognize. It was from a woman named Mindy who worked in college admin with my cousin and had posted about our search for a surrogate on Facebook. She was twenty-nine, and since she and her husband had had their first child the previous year, she'd been thinking about surrogacy.

'Having Charlotte was one of the most important things I've done,' she wrote. 'I really want to help someone who can't do that experience that for themselves.' She was okay with the fact that we didn't have embryos, and she knew miscarriage was still a possibility. Her husband and mother supported her, and when Jeremy and I met them all, we felt not only a rush of relief at how kind and trustworthy they seemed; but also a shock of familiarity at their dynamics: the dark-humoured banter between Mindy and her husband, Eric – so much like mine and Jeremy's – their love of animals, the fact that they'd named their daughter Charlotte Elizabeth – the name we'd had for years on our list of name for girls. As the four of us sat in their living room and agreed to go forward, Charlotte popped up and down over the edge of her playpen, peering at me, like a tiny firecracker with pigtails shooting straight up from her head.

We also found Anna, our egg donor, online. I loved her immediately, not only because she had thick reddish hair like an Alphonse Mucha illustration and shared my taste in books and art, but because she was willing to have an open, known relationship with any children we had using her eggs – something that was important to us. She had initially donated eggs for the money – around $10,000 – but seeing the twins created from her prior donation had since made her excited about the possibility of helping create families. Going from my own eggs to hers was initially an easy decision. Many women I knew had taken years to warm up to the idea of using donor eggs, but unlike them, I had the advantage of having been stubbornly disinterested in my own DNA. I had always been uncurious about the branching family trees my aunt put together; I had never fantasized about seeing my mother's eyes or my grandfather's grin on my own child. Still, as we moved toward the reality of it, I felt new grief. Not so much for the loss of my genetics, but for the total loss of a conventional motherhood story. False as it may be, for many people, mothers are people with both a genetic and gestational connection to their children – certainly at least one of the two. Using Anna's eggs in addition to Mindy's uterus made my parenthood so different from that of most women, I worried I'd always feel different and alone. But after Anna completed her egg retrieval and we started texting, I felt a relief and pride at my new connection that mostly outweighed my anxiety. In one sense, as with Mindy's, Anna's presence didn't diminish my motherhood, but added to it: I had another partner in the process.

By the fall, Jeremy and I had nine frozen embryos, but, eager as we were, the gravity of the situation hadn't fully impressed itself on me. Jeremy, Mindy, Eric, and I slogged through the routine of clearing medical, legal, and psychological screening, and then the wrenching process of shipping embryos to Toronto, thawing the best one, and, after she'd undergone a trying regime of injections and monitoring, transferring it to Mindy's uterus. It worked on the first try. But as the pregnancy went on, each blood test promising, each series of heartbeats measured and deemed perfect in frequency and strength, I had to accept something multiple losses had made seem impossible: we were having a baby. In gaps in my days, I found myself saying this to myself silently, over and over, like a mantra: *We're having a baby*. But the excitement wasn't there, just relief that he was still alive, that this one wasn't dead yet. And as long as he was alive, I would not have to keep trying for him. Waiting for my baby felt less like anticipation than a break from prolonged effort and pain.

Mindy, her belly rounding, her cheeks flushed with hormones, was the site of this break, the space in which I located my relief. I saw the baby inside her – I saw him on ultrasounds, his nose sharply upturned, his spine a delicate puzzle in the translucent skin. Every week, his fist was raised up by his face, and we'd joke that already he was a very political, very left-wing baby. What I couldn't feel of him, Mindy narrated: he kicked a lot, mostly at night, and he moved around when he heard music, or she'd play Jeremy's and my voices for him using headphones she'd stick on her belly. Every visit, he was more and more present, pushing Mindy's belly out the front of her parka, making it difficult for her to sit or run. But despite these signs of life, he was still mostly a theory, an idea. The baby that hadn't died yet.

'Since he's still alive, maybe I can start buying things,' I rationalized, when he was still a few months away. I bought onesies with prints of ponies and hamburgers and a big soft toy bunny, because years ago I'd seen a little curly-haired boy holding one, in a dream. I put the things in the Room, the room that every infertile couple has, the one that is supposed to be for a baby, then fills with sad junk, until (if) luck changes. I moved around some of the junk and spread out the new cute things. But it still didn't look like stuff for a real baby, in a room for a person that would actually exist. It felt provisional – stuff for a baby that hadn't died yet.

A familiar pattern of anxiety for an infertile parent-to-be, but luckily the baby himself would have none of it. He came five weeks early and quick as a flash flood, before Mindy's epidural had a chance to work, and while Jeremy was in line at a Walmart, hurriedly buying a car seat. *But I haven't even processed this yet*, went a line in my head. *He was still just an idea!* It didn't matter, I realized, because the baby didn't care, and the baby was here. I had spent years lamenting how invisible I felt in my infertility, how little understood, but in truth, no one would ever be more indifferent to my neuroses than my newly born son. No one cares less about your trauma than a baby. But how quickly he eclipsed it, too, and us, and everything else. He changed so much in those first few minutes: at first just a head between Mindy's thighs, then a wiggling eel, yellowish, laid down on her belly. Then, wiped down, a squalling red silhouette with a rubbery cord I cut myself and the doctor clamped with a plastic clip. Then a series of measurements – six pounds! twenty inches! – that the doctor shouted into the room from the tiny basin in which the newborn was prodded and measured. The room collectively sighed: despite being born premature, he was healthy and robust, and wouldn't need NICU. Then, finally, a tiny little baby in a diaper that a nurse laid between my bare chest and my hospital gown: silent suddenly. Sleeping.

Apparently I was crying so hard I could barely stand – I don't remember that. What I remember is the screaming red child, the way the exact pitch of his voice had an immediate and indescribable meaning to me, the way he plugged into my chest in a very exact and deliberate way and instantly fell asleep.

At some point, Jeremy returned from Walmart. I looked at him. *We had a baby*. His name was Charlie, and he was sleeping on my chest. Jeremy put his arms around both of us. Across the room, doctors adjusted beeping machines around Mindy while Eric cradled her head and her mother held her hand. Off to her side was the placenta, bloody and beached, doctors picking through it. In my infertility groups, people often described surrogates as angels, but with her slick skin and the tubes twisting off her like seaweed, she looked more like a mermaid, and the air smelled damp and old.

Eventually, Mindy turned her head and we caught each other's eye. Oh, I thought. This is what she wanted me to have. This is what she was talking about. The fact of this: that there was so great a feeling I had not known – and that another woman had been willing to give it to me – overwhelmed me as much as Charlie's existence. Mindy and I looked at each other for a few moments, breathing.

Later, the nurses guided me, Jeremy, and Charlie into our own room. The hospital had not been prepared for our labour team of four, but had found a space for us with twin beds, between which they wedged a bassinet for Charlie. But these provisions were mostly moot; no one slept for a good forty-eight hours, so constant was the care of this tiny body. His demands were a punishing combination of frequent and random – there was no way to predict the next task, despite it being always either feeding, changing, burping, or holding him. The physical and primal labour was impossible to stream-line or hack – a kind of ur-work. The only thing to really do was to surrender to it, to let our big adult world contract to a tiny star and orbit Planet Charlie.

Mindy had been given a room down the hall to recover in the company of Eric and her mother. When Charlie would let me, I thought about her, about the nice symmetry of the moment, each family in an identical room, her labour ending as mine had begun. A common second-wave feminist objection to surrogacy (as well as for C-sections and drugged labour) was that it separates motherhood from the bodily work of pregnancy and childbirth. I already knew this was bullshit. The medical experience of my infertility – all the miscarriages, surgeries, tests, and IVF, as well as the physical burden of the attendant grief – was as much a part of the process of conceiving Charlie as Anna's egg retrieval or Mindy's pregnancy. (*This is my labour*, I said to myself after every surgery.) But I was less prepared for how bodily early motherhood was, how the combination of fatigue and a newborn baby would produce an effect that was hormonal – almost postpartum. My stomach cramped; I was sweating buckets. Most surprisingly, my breasts were sore. Curious, I let Charlie latch and suckle, and immediately felt milk pull down to my nipple. The nurse told me that, having been pregnant multiple times, I already had the plumbing to produce breast milk, and now my body was responding hormonally to the proximity of a baby. Jeremy, too, got folded into this biome, a three-person constant exchange of touch and skin and hormone-steeped sweat; soon we all smelled the same, like slightly sour breast milk. I did not need to go through labour to learn – as all new mothers do – that the term *labour* is an insulting misnomer that implies it ends after birth.

There was also a loneliness in this closeness, but it wasn't until the day after we were discharged, when we had to return to the hospital for a hellish early-morning checkup, that I was able to touch it. I missed *them*. For over a year, Eric and Mindy had become entwined in Jeremy's and my lives in a way no other two people had. We not only made Charlie together, but we had become friends. New parents themselves, they had become our sherpas to the journey of not only having, but also raising, a baby. Few days had gone by when Mindy and I weren't constantly texting about parent stuff: what to buy and what wasn't worth it; what various dramatic personae in the Canadian surrogacy world had said or done online that day; the ridiculous pressures mothers faced in a 'mommy culture' of brand-sponsored Instagram posts of $20,000 nurseries and strollers with four iPhone chargers (or whatever). As delighted as I was to have Charlie back in Toronto with us, shrinking our parenting team of four down to two was disorienting. When we saw Mindy and Eric at Charlie's checkup, bearing a cooler of pumped colostrum, I felt my unease melt. Online, I'd been advised frequently by other parents to not continue a relationship with a surrogate because I might feel intimidated by another mother figure in my baby's life. We had an open relationship with Anna, but the connection between Mindy and Charlie was more immediate and intimate, and thus more potentially threatening. But it never felt right to me to sever it, and now I knew for sure we weren't doing that. Charlie had knit us together.

And yet, even this flourish of optimism germinated from that familiar black seed: all the miscarriages, the years and years of grief. Some people say the condition of modern womanhood is one of navigating contradictions and clashes: between the personal and the political, the said and the done, the body and the heart. For me, every time I saw Mindy, or Charlie, or even Jeremy, and every time I texted with Anna, I was aware of two stories, the one in which I had to have other women help make my baby (how sad!) and the one in which I got to have a baby with other women (pretty cool!).

Was this a feminist experience? I wasn't sure. One of the reasons women in my infertility groups often considered surrogacy, like adoption, a 'last resort' was that their infertility would become very public and visible, and, because they still faced so much stigma, make them extra-vulnerable. But in the weeks and months that followed Charlie's birth, I found myself trumpeting his unusual conception, hopeful that by being so public, I might start to chisel at others' discomfort with, and misconceptions about, female infertility. It was an easier time than ever to be loud: infertility was having a moment in the press. Some of the most revered pop feminist celebrities, including Chrissy Teigan (my favourite), Beyoncé, and Kim Kardashian, were opening up about their struggles with miscarriage and infertility, as well as their experiences with IVF, while gay men such as Elton John, Tom Ford, and at least one of the new *Queer Eye* guys were proudly building families through egg donation and surrogacy. Articles about infertility ran in almost every publication, including parenting magazines and websites. TV shows were addressing the topic in ways that were surprisingly nuanced: for example, Tyra Banks's character on the show *Black-ish*, a new mom after infertility, who confesses that 'when you've tried this hard to have a baby, you think you have no right to complain.' (Banks is herself infertile and had recently had her first child via surrogacy – I imagined she had something to do with this bit of dialogue.) Screens were full of it: the CBC web series by Wendy Litner, *How to Buy a Baby*, based on the writer's own experiences with IVF (Litner subsequently became a mother via adoption); the beautifully told documentary *Vegas Baby*, about a queer single woman trying to conceive via donor eggs and sperm; and *Private Life*, a drama about a couple struggling with the aftermath of failed fertility treatments and an unsuccessful adoption. Social media was beginning to provide a welcome alternative to infertility support groups, with Twitter feeds (my favourite: a man with azoospermia who tweets as Balls Don't Work [@gotnosperm]), Instagrammers, and Tumblr bloggers using imagery and humour to express not only their personal grief, but the often-messy politics of infertility. In the U.K., 2018 saw the launch of Fertility Fest, an arts festival devoted to the topic of infertility and modern reproduction. Many stories, such as Michelle Obama's disclosure that her daughters were born after a miscarriage and IVF, spurred a long-overdue conversation about infertility and race.

Activists were also making news: in 2016, the Human Rights Tribunal of Ontario decided in favour of a Markham woman who was fired from her job after suffering depression related to a pregnancy loss, issuing a decision that could ulti-mately redefine miscarriage as a disability. The same year, the World Health Organization added single people of all genders, as well as couples in same-sex relationships, to their definition of infertility, arguing that they deserved equal access to reproductive health services, including reproductive technologies such as IVF, under their home countries' health-care programs. WHO argued that infertile people, as well as people in non-reproductive circumstances (like being single or in a same-sex partnership), deserve the 'right to reproduce' – a declaration that ultimately expands the idea of 'reproductive rights' beyond the negative rights to abortion and birth control.

All of this pop visibility is notable because it's mostly being done by infertile women themselves, going beyond either the shallow mandate of 'raising awareness,' as in health journalism from the early 2000s, or the faint fascination-repulsion of current reporting on reproductive technology. It showed that infertility is work: the work of grief, the blood and sweat of medical treatment, and the labour of having to deal with the misapprehensions and biases of the fertile world, while also going through treatment and/or grief. It linked up, I thought, with a larger movement toward displaying the gritty, often ugly work of motherhood, displaying how, for us, trying to have a baby is also a type of maternal labour, a body-and-soul sacrifice for the child who is yet to come. It weaves us into a larger, feminist-friendly narrative about motherhood as work that is itself long overdue.

In humanizing infertility, these pop representations also normalize it and, by extension, the reality of treatment in the for-profit infertility industry, a sphere that remains widely – and mostly correctly – criticized by many feminist scholars and writers. It doesn't escape me that in the first-person accounts of infertility I had started seeing in entertainment and news media over the past few years, undergoing IVF, or considering surrogacy or donor sperm or eggs, was presented as an inevitable part of being infertile. This is undoubtedly true to these persons' experiences, but it also runs a risk – not only of downplaying the fact that many of these procedures are still largely experimental, poorly regulated, often unsuccessful, and rife with serious side-effects for female patients specifically, but of folding reproductive technology into a larger, neo-liberal feminist project that sees family-building as a consumer choice.

Alana Cattapan, a feminist historian who documents the history of assisted reproductive technology legislation in Canada, has argued that the creation of the private ART industry in the West mirrored and entrenched the idea of 'reproductive citizenship' in neo-liberal society: a person whose rights to reproduce, or not reproduce, are enabled by their access to free-market biomedical resources, such as birth control, abortion, and technologies like IVF. Legislation, such as the Assisted Human Reproduction Act (the same one with which Jeremy, Mindy, and I had to contend to have Charlie), worked not only to legitimize ART as a private consumer option (instead of a health-care issue to be folded into public health-care plans), but to define who did, and who did not, count as a 'reproductive citizen.' Ultimately – and unsurprisingly, given the paucity of feminist voices on the committees that shaped the act – reproductive citizenship was afforded to infertile, straight, middle-class Canadians, while the interests of LGBTQ Canadians, third parties such as surrogates and egg/sperm donors, and the children born of these technologies were marginalized. (For example, only one surrogate was consulted in drafting the policy around surrogacy, and the legislation around sperm donation allows donors to remain anonymous, to the ongoing protest of many children born of donor sperm.)

By privileging the interests of infertile straight couples with money, Cattapan argues, reproductive technology was used to uphold the patriarchal idea of the two-parent, genetically linked, heterosexual family. In her dissertation on the topic, she writes:

> The interests of infertile Canadians did not fundamentally challenge family norms, or the importance of biological ties; rather they reiterated the importance of having one's own children within the context of a nuclear, heterosexual family. Infertile Canadians were seeking out the fulfillment of conventional Canadian family life, only they needed to use ARTs to do so.

This reflects a distinction I had long noted in the surrogacy community specifically, where infertile women seeking surrogacy were consumed by the possibility of recreating the typical conception as much as possible – making the surrogacy feel as close to 'actually being pregnant' themselves as the situation could allow – while LGBTQ parents-to-be tended to embrace the situation as a whole new way to have babies, a step into the unknown.

Back home, still knit to Mindy but feeling increasingly snug in our pod of three, I spend time in between feedings reading about these families (Charlie strapped on my chest as I hold my phone above his head – the consummate pose of new motherhood in the digital age). The most radical families were born from a technology designed to uphold patriarchal convention. Andrew Solomon has a rambling, widely-flung-but-still-close family composed of kids conceived with his sperm but raised by lesbian parents, a child with his partner conceived through egg donation and surrogacy, and a stepchild via his partner's former spouse. Michelle Tea, an infertile queer woman who carried and birthed her son, who was conceived with an egg from her partner, who is transmasculine, and donor sperm. Or, closer to home, a single, gay man in my IVF group who is conceiving with a donated embryo and his sister as a surrogate, or my friend Victoria, a surrogate who has carried two children for a gay couple she remains close to in an 'auntie' role, and is currently considering a traditional surrogacy (her egg, their sperm) for two men, one of whom is living with HIV (she will be called the child's 'surrogate mother'). I used to think the transhumanist theory of Donna Haraway – in which the marginalized appropriate technology to create new ways of being, and new patterns of kinship, identities, and language (one of Solomon's kids calls him 'doughnut dad,' a riff on 'donor dad') – was overly utopian, but it was basically already happening. In a Haraway cyborg world, children like Charlie, with his multiple mothers and his biotechnical conception, were not objects of pity but harbingers of a more equitable world, in which the pleasures and risks of family were available to all. Writes Solomon:

> I espouse reproductive libertarianism, because when everyone has the broadest choice, love itself expands. The affection my family have found in one another is not a better love, but it is another love, and just as species diversity is crucial to sustain the planet, this diversity strengthens the ecosphere of kindness. The road less travelled by, as it turns out, leads to pretty much the same place … I wonder whether I would have found as much joy in marriage and children if they had come easily – if I had been straight or had grown up 30 years later in a somewhat more welcoming society. Perhaps I would; perhaps all the complex imagining I've had to do could have been applied to broader endeavours. I believe, however, that the struggle

has given me a vision as a parent that I would not have had without it. So much of me had been consecrated to loneliness, and now I am not lonely any more. Now, children make me happy. A generation ago, this love would have stayed dormant and unrealised.

As feminists like Cattapan have pointed out, ART is conceived of and managed as yet another reproductive choice for straight couples to participate in normative heterosexual life. But for feminists to respond to this reality by calling for outright restrictions on the technology, or restrictions on commercialization without accounting for the fact that all our labour is commercialized, is simplistic and risky. It blunts its most radical and most feminist possibilities: that we could use these technologies to expand our definitions of family and motherhood in ways that benefit all the people involved.

A few weeks after Charlie was born, I found myself going back to my old IVF and surrogacy message boards, wondering what these communities of women could have been like had there been even a vague feminist ethos. If earlier feminists had seen us as sisters, rather than patriarchal dupes or oppressors of other women. If infertility lobby groups had embraced an idea of infertility as an issue of medical, emotional, and spiritual health, rather than a type of consumer identity. I imagined a feminist movement parallel to the one for abortion access, in which women would call for more research into the causes of infertility, the potential efficacies of various treatments, as well as their risks. We could call for expanded access to proven reproductive health care for all Canadians – not just the rich ones, not just those in cities who are partnered and straight – by demanding it be brought under the auspices of a properly regulated health-care system. We could align ourselves with, rather than against, surrogates and egg donors, lobbying for a system in which policies around third-party reproduction are shaped by them, for their own safety and interests, opening up the possibility of them organizing as workers. We could support infertile women who do not conceive in either finding other forms of family or healing into satisfying lives lived without children. Truly patient-centric clinics could bloom under our watch. Perhaps most importantly, infertile feminists could embrace our status as different kinds of women – as the kinds of women who eat people in folk tales and get thrown down elevators in movies – to challenge the idea that motherhood is unthinking, automatic, and instinctual, and be living examples of how maternity is instead a thing that is both worked at and worked for, sometimes by multiple people, and sometimes not by women at all.

I scrolled through the boards, the endless posts about follicle counts and sperm fragmentation and beta results, the proffers of 'Hang in there' and wishes of baby dust, and thought I should add something like this, but then the baby started whimpering, and my mother was coming over soon, and within a few minutes I'd forgotten, sucked back into the routine of feeding-then-changing-then-holding Charlie, who still couldn't care less about whatever pointless debate I was planning on social media. What a creature he was. The incredible muchness of my many-mothered child. His multipronged roots of will and optimism, and shit-tons of money, and advanced science, and – quite deep down now – that black seed of longing and loss.

Much is born from less.

Endnotes

1. When I saw *Baby Mama* in the theatre in 2008, the diagnosis seemed like an innocuous detail; when I rewatched it during my own surrogacy experience, I was so shocked I had to pause the video and check IMDB's description of the movie to see if I had actually heard what I thought I had. In a series of zingers, the movie implies that Kate's condition is due to drugs she was exposed to in utero in the 1970s, a clear analogue to DES syndrome, a constellation of reproductive deformities in women whose mothers were prescribed the powerful anti-nausea drug DES during pregnancy. Many 'DES daughters,' as they are known, are at increased risk for breast cancer and rare cancers of the reproductive tract; others suffer disabling autoimmune conditions; and a great many experience infertility or multiple miscarriages (surrogacy is an oft-prescribed and largely successful option for these women, a detail the movie actually got right). That Fey would present such a devastating and dangerous condition so cavalierly, as something that is not really a big deal but also hilarious, in my opinion, moved *Baby Mama* out of the category of predictably offensive to outright ableist and dehumanizing, even by Hollywood illness-narrative standards.

2. As in antiquity, where the only first-person accounts of female infertility are registered in their offerings to oracles and gods, the best glimpse we have of infertile women in the Edwardian era is in the artifacts of their desperation: the lucrative cottage industry of quack nostrums, salves, and tinctures marketed for 'barrenness.' The explosion of folk remedies, accelerated by the new consumer culture and bolstered by the growth of print advertising, was such a threat to the institution of medicine that the British Medical Association twice attempted – in 1909 and 1912 – to convince the government to legislate them.

3. But one example: Michelle Tea, a queer writer in progressive Los Angeles, documented for *Autostraddle* the subtle microaggressions she faced while undergoing IVF with her trans partner – for example, the exhausting routine of having to constantly correct the clinic about her partner's gender.

Works Cited

Baby Mama. Dir. Michael McCullers. Relativity Media: 2008.

Bane, Theresa. *Encyclopedia of Spirits and Ghosts in World Mythology.* Jefferson, NC: McFarland, 2016.

Basen, Gwynne et al., eds. *Misconceptions.* Hull: Voyageur Publishing, 1993.

Baskin, Judith R. *Midrashic Women: Formations of the Feminine in Rabbinic Literature.* Brandeis UP, 2005.

Bell, Ann V. *Misconception: Social Class and Infertility in America.* New Jersey: Rutgers, 2014.

Bhattacharji, Sukumari. 'Motherhood in Ancient India.' *Economic and Political Weekly* 25, no. 42/43 (1990): WS50-S57.www.jstor.org/stable/4396892.

Boggs, Belle. *The Art of Waiting: On Fertility, Medicine, and Motherhood.* Minneapolis: Graywolf, 2016.

Brown, Sherronda J. 'The Handmaid's Tale and the Reproductive Rights Movement's White Supremacy Problem.' AFROPUNK. Accessed December 01, 2018. http://afropunk.com/tag/gaze/.

Butler, Judith. (2003) 'Violence, Mourning, Politics.' *Studies in Gender and Sexuality,* 4:1, 9-37

Cattapan, Alana. 'Controlling Conception: Citizenship and the Governance of Assisted Reproductive Technologies in Canada (1989-2004).' Dissertation, York University, 2015.

Chen, T. H., et al. 'Prevalence of Depressive and Anxiety Disorders in an Assisted Reproductive Technique Clinic.' *Human Reproduction,* 2004; 19:2313–2318.

Christian Life Resources. (2018). *As God Wills: Understanding God's Plan for Childless Couples.* [online] Available at: https://christianliferesources.com/2018/05/08/as-god-wills-understanding-gods-plan-for-childless-couples/ [Accessed 1 Dec. 2018].

Conybeare, F. C. 'The Testament of Solomon.' *Jewish Quarterly Review,* Vol. 11, No. 1 (October 1898), pp. 1–45. University of Pennsylvania Press. Accessed: 25 September 2018. www.jstor.org/stable/1450398.

Corea, Gena. *The Mother Machine: From Artificial Insemination to Artificial Wombs.* New York: Harper and Row, 1985.

Domar, AD, Friedman R, and Zuttermeister PC. 1993. 'The psychological impact of infertility: a comparison with patients with other medical conditions.' *Journal of Psychosomatic Obstetrics & Gynecology.* 14 (Suppl.) 45-52.

Dow, Joseph. 'History of the Town of Hampton, New Hampshire: From its Settlement in 1638 to the Autumn of 1892.' Vol. 1. Hampton: Salem Press Publishing and Printing Company, 1894.

Epstein, Rachel. 'Married, Single, or Gay? Queerying and Trans-Forming the Practices of Assisted Human Reproduction Services.' Dissertation, York University, 2014.

'Examining the Congruence Between Couples' Infertility-Related Stress and Its Relationship to Depression and Marital Adjustment in Infertile Men and Women. Peterson, B. D. et al. *Fertility and Sterility*, Vol. 76 , Issue 3, S25–S26.

Faludi, Susan. Backlash: *The Undeclared War Against American Women*. New York: Three Rivers Press, 2006.

Fatal Attraction. Dir. Adrian Lyne. Paramount Pictures, 1987.

FINRRAGE-UBINIG International Conference, 'Reproductive and Genetic Engineering and Women's Reproductive Health.' Comilla, Bangladesh, March 1989. Accessed 25 September 2018, www.finrrage.org/wp-content/uploads/2016/03/International_News.pdf.

Firestone, Shulamith. *The Dialectic of Sex: The Case for Feminist Revolution*. New York: Morrow, 1970.

Friedan, Betty. *The Feminine Mystique*. New York: Norton, 1963.

Godbeer, Richard. *The Devil's Dominion: Magic and Religion in Early New England*. Cambridge: Cambridge UP, 1994.

Goldman, Emma. *Anarchy and the Sex Question: Essays on Women and Emancipation, 1896-1926*. Shawn P. Wilbur, ed. Oakland, CA: PM Press, 2016.

Greer, Germaine. *Sex and Destiny*. London: Secker and Warburg, 1984.

Hall, Stephen S. 'IVF: A New Last Chance.' *The Cut, New York Magazine*. September 18, 2017. Accessed 25 September 2018. medium.com/the-cut/ivf-a-new-last-chance-6896baeaf1ff.

The Handmaid's Tale. Bruce Miller, creator. MGM Television, 2017. Netflix.

Herrera, Hayden. *Frida: A Biography of Frida Kahlo*. New York: Perennial, 2002.

Hjelmstedt, A., L. et al. 'Gender Differences in Psychological Reactions to Infertility Among Couples Seeking IVF and ICSI Treatment.' *Acta Obstetricia et Gynecologica Scandinavica*, 78: 42-49, 1999.

'Infertility Is a Reproductive Justice Issue." *Boricua Feminist*. January 30, 2018. Accessed December 01, 2018. https://boricuafeminist.com/2018/01/infertility-is-a-reproductive-justice-issue/.

Kahlo, Frida. 'Frida and the Miscarriage.' Paper. 1932. Retrieved from artsandculture.google.com/asset/frida-and-the-miscarriage/3gFXDanEJcmRJA?hl=en.

Kahlo, Frida. Henry Ford Hospital. Painting. 1932. Retrieved from artsandculture.google.com/asset/henry-ford-hospital/kgHTa-02kVhHJA?hl=en.

Kelly, Amita. 'Fact Check: Was Planned Parenthood Started To "Control" The Black Population?' NPR. August 14, 2015. Accessed December 01, 2018. https://www.npr.org/sections/itsallpolitics/2015/08/14/432080520/fact-check-was-planned-parenthood-started-to-control-the-black-population.

Klein, Renate. *Surrogacy: A Human Rights Violation*. North Melbourne: Spinifex, 2017.

Lakatos, Enikő et al. 'Anxiety and Depression among Infertile Women: A Cross-Sectional Survey from Hungary.' *BMC Women's Health* 17 (2017): 48. PMC. Accessed 25 September 2018.

Layne, Linda L. *Motherhood Lost: A Feminist Account of Pregnancy Loss in America*. New York: Routledge, 2003.

Levy, Ariel. 'Catherine Opie, All-American Subversive.' *New Yorker*. March 13, 2017. Accessed 25 September 2018. www.newyorker.com/magazine/2017/03/13/catherine-opie-all-american-subversive.

Lichy, Erle. 'Demons and Population Control.' *Expedition Magazine*. 13.2 (1971). Penn Museum 1971. Accessed 01 Dec 2018. https://www.penn.museum/sites/expedition/demons-and-population-control/

Little, Shelagh. 'Life After Infertility Treatments Fail.' *New York Times*. September 10, 2009. Accessed 28 January 2018. parenting.blogs.nytimes.com/2009/09/10/life-after-infertility-treatments-fail/

Lublin, Nancy. *Pandora's Box: Feminism Confronts Reproductive Technology*. Lanham: Rowman & Littlefield, 1998.

Mahjouri, Nadia. 'Techno-Maternity: Rethinking the Possibilities of Reproductive Technologies.' *Thirdspace: A Journal of Feminist Theory* 4 (2004).

McGuire, Linda H. 'From Greek Myth to Medieval Witches: Infertile Women as Monstrous and Evil.' Proceedings of At the *Interface*. Sorcha Ni Fhlainn, ed. Oxford: Inter-Disciplinary Press, 2010, 136–51.

Merrick, Janna C. *The Politics of Pregnancy: Policy Dilemmas in the Maternal- Fetal Relationship*. Abingdon: Routledge, 2014.

Midelfort, H. C. Erik, *Witch Hunting in Southwestern Germany, 1562-1684: The Social and Intellectual Foundations*. California: Stanford UP, 1972.

Mies, Maria. 'Why Do We Need All This? A Call Against Genetic Engineering and Reproductive Technology.' *Women's Studies International Forum*, Vol. 8, Issue 6, 1985. 553–60.

Mills, Catherine. *Futures of Reproduction: Bioethics and Biopolitics*. International Library of Ethics, Law, and the New Medicine. New York: Springer, 2011.

Moss, Gabrielle. 'Why The "Biological Clock" To Have Kids Is A Myth.' [online] *Bustle*. March 8, 2016. Available at: https://www.bustle.com/articles/146600-why-womens-biological-clock-ticking-is-actually-a-total-myth [Accessed 1 Dec. 2018].

National Action Committee on the Status of Women. *New Reproductive Technologies: A Technological Handmaid's Tale*. Toronto, October 1990.

Nelson, Maggie. *The Argonauts*. Minneapolis: Graywolf, 2015.

Ngozi Adichie, Chimamanda. 'The Danger of a Single Story.' TED. 2009. Lecture.

O'Callahan, Tiffany. 'Infertility May Increase Risk of Mental Disorders.' *New Scientist*, July 12, 2012. www.newscientist.com/article/dn22020-infertility-may-increase-risk-of-mental-disorders/.

Opie, Catherine. *Self Portrait/Cutting*. Photograph. 1993, Retrieved from artsandculture.google.com/asset/self-portrait-cutting/yQG2x2FpePzJXw?hl=en.

———. *Self Portrait/Pervert*. Photograph. 1993. Retrieved from artsandculture.google.com/asset/self-portrait-pervert/sAEjsF6pf5XOHQ?hl=en.

———. *Self Portrait/Nursing*. Photograph. 2004. Retrieved from www.guggenheim.org/artwork/14666.

Pfeffer, Naomi, and Anne Woollett. *The Experience of Infertility*. London: Virago, 1983.

Pfeffer, Naomi. *The Stork and the Syringe: A Political History of Reproductive Medicine*. Cambridge: Polity Press, 1993.

Purkiss, Diane. *The Witch in History*. London: Routledge, 1996.

Raymond, Janice G. *Women as Wombs: Reproductive Technologies and the Battle Over Women's Freedom*. North Melbourne: Spinifex, 1994.

Rothman Katz, Barbara. 'The Products of Conception: The social context of reproductive choices.' *Journal of Medical Ethics* (11), 1985, 188-192. Accessed 01 Dec 18. https://jme.bmj.com/content/medethics/11/4/188.full.pdf

Ruddick, Sara. *Maternal Thinking: Toward a Politics of Peace*. Boston: Beacon Press, 1989.

Sanger, Margaret. 'America Needs a Code for Babies.' *American Weekly*, March 27, 1934. Margaret Sanger Papers, Library of Congress, 128:0312B. Accessed 2 September 2018, www.nyu.edu/projects/sanger/webedition/app/documents/show.php?sangerDoc=101807.xml.

———. 'Morality and Birth Control.' *Birth Control Review* 11, February-March 1918. Margaret Sanger Microfilm S70:793 . Accessed 25 September 2018. www.nyu.edu/projects/sanger/webedition/app/documents/show.php?sangerDoc=213391.xml.

———. *Woman and the New Race*. New York: Brentano's, 1920. Accessed 25 September 2018, www.gutenberg.org/ebooks/8660.

Serano, Julia. *Whipping Girl: A Transsexual Woman on Sexism and the Scapegoating of Femininity*. Berkeley: Seal Press, 2007.

Shivanandan, Mary. 'Women and ART.' *Humanum Review*. Summer 2012. Accessed Dec 01, 2018. humanumreview.com/articles/women-and-art.

Simonds, Wendy, and Barbara Katz Rothman. *Centuries of Solace: Expressions of Maternal Grief in Popular Literature*. Philadelphia: Temple UP, 1992.

Solanas, Valerie. *SCUM Manifesto*. London: Verso, 2004.

Solomon, Andrew. *Far from the Tree: Parents, Children, and the Search for Identity*. New York: Scribner, 2012.

Stabile, Carol A. *Feminism and the Technological Fix*. New York: Manchester UP, 1994.

Steinberg, Deborah Lynn, and Patricia Spallone, eds. *Made to Order: The Myth of Reproductive and Genetic Progress*. New York: Teacher's College Press: 1992.

Stevens, Angi Becker. 'What Is Reproductive Justice?' *Solidarity*. Accessed December 01, 2018. https://solidarity-us.org/atc/188/p4971/.

Stopes, Marie Carmichael. *Radiant Motherhood: A Book for Those Who Are Creating the Future*. London: GP Putnam's Sons, 1920. Accessed 25 September 2018, archive.org/details/radiantmotherhoooostopuoft.

The Hand That Rocks the Cradle. Dir. Curtis Hanson. Buena Vista Pictures: 1992.

The Holy Bible: King James Version. Dallas: Brown Books Publishing, 2004.

Thomsell, Michael C. *Heresy in the Roman Catholic Church*. Jefferson, NC: McFarland, 2011. Volgsten, H., et al. 'Prevalence of Psychiatric Disorders in Infertile Women and Men Undergoing in Vitro Fertilization Treatment.' *Human Reproduction* (Oxford, England) 23.9 (2008): 2056–2063. PMC. Web. 25 September 2018.

'The Baby Show.' *30 Rock*. NBC. New York. January 4, 2007. Television.

'Winona Ryder/Moby.' *Saturday Night Live*. NBC. New York. May 18, 2002. Television.

Weigel, Moira. 'We Live in the Reproductive Dystopia of "The Handmaid's Tale."' *The New Yorker*. June 19, 2017. Accessed December 01, 2018. https://www.newyorker.com/books/page-turner/we-live-in-the-reproductive-dystopia-of-the-handmaids-tale.

Woolf, Virginia. *On Being Ill*. Ashfield, Mass: Paris Press, 2012.

Zarzycka, Marta Joanna. *Body as Crisis: Representation of Pain in Visual Arts*. Utrecht University, 2007.

Acknowledgements

Beloved Jeremy, Charles, Mom, Dad, Peter, Gabrielle: you are the most supportive, inspiring, and beautiful family a writer could ask for. My gratitude to you goes beyond bounds.

Mindy, Eric, Charlotte, Anna, and Robert – you are the proverbial village in which my family thrives; I hope you see this book as the celebration of you that it fundamentally is.

Amy, Ana, Linsay, Heather, Bethany, Ben, Scott, Brittany-Lyne, Coko, Cathy – you are splendid humans and superlative friends.

Sarah Sahagian, Alanna Cattapan, Charlotte Shane, and Varda Burstyn, of all the experts I interviewed for this project, you went above and beyond to ensure that I had accurate and relevant information. I am grateful for your participation, the challenge of feminist debate, and the opportunity to change and grow.

Thomas Hannam, Charles March, and Richard Marrs –if only all techno-patriarchs invested in the medico-capitalistic exploitation of womanhood were as compassionate, talented and supportive as you! Thank you for helping us make our baby.

Emily Keeler – this could not have been an easy story to help tell. But you did so with the utmost compassion as well as commitment to the book's overall intellectual integrity and impact. You are a brilliant editor, thinker, ally, and friend.

David Reed, Priscila Uppal, Matthew Rowlinson, Matthew McKinnon, Alexandra Molotkow, and Sarah Fulford – as with everything I write, this book is rooted in your mentorship.

Elizabeth Kimball: wherever you are, I hope someone can hook you up with a (gin!) martini and a supernatural copy of this little book. I think you will be bored but proud.

About the Author

Alexandra Kimball is a writer and editor in Toronto. She is a seven-time National Magazine Award nominee. Her journalism and essays appear regularly in major publications across Canada, including *Chatelaine, The Walrus, Flare,* and *Reader's Digest*. She is currently Associate Editor at *Toronto Life* magazine.

Typeset in Aldus Nova and Gibson Pro.

Printed at the old Coach House on bpNichol Lane in Toronto, Ontario, on Rolland Opaque Natural paper, which was manufactured, acid-free, in Saint-Jérôme, Quebec, from 50 percent recycled paper, and it was printed with vegetable-based ink on a 1972 Heidelberg KORD offset litho press. Its pages were folded on a Baumfolder, gathered by hand, bound on a Sulby Auto-Minabinda, and trimmed on a Polar single-knife cutter.

Edited by Emily M. Keeler
Cover illustration by Chloe Cushman
Author photo by Paul Terefenko
Cover design and series template designed by Ingrid Paulson

Exploded Views is a series of probing, provocative essays that offer surprising perspectives on the most intriguing cultural issues and figures of our day. Longer than a typical magazine article but shorter than a full-length book, these are punchy salvos written by some of North America's most lyrical journalists and critics. Spanning a variety of forms and genres – history, biography, polemic, commentary – and published simultaneously in digital formats and handsome, collectible print editions, this is literary reportage that at once investigates, illuminates, and intervenes. www.chbooks.com/explodedviews

Coach House Books
80 bpNichol Lane
Toronto ON M5S 3J4
Canada

416 979 2217
800 367 6360

mail@chbooks.com
www.chbooks.com

31901064632062